SELMA EVANS

THE EFFECT OF ADHD ON RELATIONSHIPS

UNDERSTANDING AND LOVING A PARTNER WITH ATTENTION DEFICIT HYPERACTIVITY DISORDER, BREAKING THROUGH BARRIERS AND STRENGTHENING YOUR RELATIONSHIP

TABLE OF CONTENTS

INTRODUCTION

My mission is to help the partners of people who have ADHD, or who they suspect might have it. I'm going to begin by telling two stories. Can you relate to the partner who doesn't have ADHD?

The first story is specifically for female readers. Is this person like you?

You make yourself a cup of coffee, sit down at the kitchen table and feel like crying. Then you push the mug aside and hammer the table with your fists, and scream... with no-one to hear you. He's gone off again to buy materials for a new DIY project! A project that came into his head only yesterday. Meanwhile, the house and the garden outside look like a building site: everywhere there's a project on the go. New paving for the path outside (half completed, so you have to finish your journey to the gate over the muddy earth), a column for a covered verandah (the roof and the other three columns yet to appear), a wall in the kitchen with no tiles on it (plastered, but the tiles you bought him with your money are still in boxes because they aren't the right size and must go back... someday).

Now he wants to put a sink outside at the back of his mom and dad's house. They tell him they'll pay him when he's finished. They know their son. Your money – his and yours – is tight.

...and you just found out you're pregnant! Your funny, humorous, hyperactive husband does know this, but has it sunk in that babies cost money? His parents also know, but it hasn't stopped them from accepting his offer to put in that sink.

He just can't sit still, and nothing seems to hold his attention for long. You can't sit on the sofa and watch a film together. Well, you can, but he will be looking at his phone for half of the time, and then when you make a remark ("Villain! Con-man! He deserved that"), your husband will look confused and say, "I didn't know he was the one behind it all." Your husband can't follow any long, complicated story. You see his eyes flicker, look sideways or just glaze over after thirty seconds.

In the end, you have such an argument with him that afterwards you asked him to go to marriage counseling. He looks a little hurt, but agrees. The two of you both feel stressed, and that you aren't on the same wavelength. The counselor asks a lot of questions, and came out with a shocking opinion: your husband might have ADHD: Attention Deficit/Hyperactivity Disorder. It kind of makes sense. He admits that he was totally hyperactive as a child. The counselor cautions you both that she isn't qualified to diagnose it, but that she could put you in contact with someone who can. So you go to a psychologist. After she holds a long interview with your husband, has an interview with you, and you and his parents have all completed questionnaires, the psychologist agrees. He has ADHD.

He isn't sure what to make of it. There are plans to start counseling and maybe to see a doctor for medication. Then he just forgets about all of this, and his eyes light up with a DIY project. Another ******* DIY project!

You ask yourself: What does this ADHD mean, and what hope is there for our relationship?

I want to share with you that there is hope. You can and need to understand ADHD; and through doing so, your husband. He needs to accept that he has it, he needs to understand himself, and he must learn new skills. ADHD is going to be with him for life, but he can overcome it and live a much more peaceful, focused and productive life. Your relationship can be happier, more romantic, and you can work, love and laugh together.

This is a book for the partners of people who have ADHD.

About two thirds of diagnosed sufferers of ADHD are men or boys. But contrary to what popular opinion thinks, we know that ADHD affects women and girls as well. A not-so-insignificant number of people go undiagnosed and misunderstood through life. The point of this book is not to give a professional diagnosis, but to help you after your partner has been diagnosed. Also, if you suspect that he or she has ADHD, I can give you many things to think about. You will need medical and psychological help to be certain of it, but knowing what it is and how it affects someone can help you to not make mistakes, and blame him or her – or yourself – unnecessarily.

Let's take a look at the second story. You are the male partner of a woman who has ADHD, or who is suspected of having it. Is this man like you?

You love your free-spirited, hippie girlfriend. She also drives you crazy. When she's happy and focused on something interesting like art or sustainable living, she's inspiring. At parties or gatherings, she socializes with everyone. She's artistic and has a good sense of humor.

Alas, she's the most unpractical woman you know. She could suggest to you excitedly that the two of you go to the forest park in the mountains for a picnic. You get ready, taking the food and drink, and some raincoats in case it rains. As you sit there looking up at the mountainous splendor, eating your sandwiches, she says, "Can we climb that mountain? The view up there must be amazing."

"Climb up there? You're not serious!" you say.

"But there must be a path or some kind of trail. We could go halfway, at least."

"It must be three thousand feet up to the top, and there's snow!"

"Can't we try? Just go for a walk as far as the snow."

"Gillian, you're crazy! We're wearing canvas shoes and we only have raincoats, no jerseys!"

You come home from work on day after driving through the rain for hours, and there is Gillian, sitting making dream-catchers, feathers and thread all over the place.

"Hi, home at last!" You talk together for a while, but you are totally starving, and there's no aroma of food.

"Tell me, what's for supper? Do you need to heat it up?"

"Supper? Oh... sorry, I forgot."

You are a modern boyfriend who believes in sharing chores equally. You cook and clean, wash and hang out the clothes, all the rest. Yet this was Gillian's turn to cook. It's too late to buy a take-away meal (which neither of you like because you know what's in them) and you're in no mood to wait for her to cook, or to help her... which you'd need to do to speed things up. Sandwiches again! Nagging (so she doesn't forget things or events) and sighing with frustration (when she does yet again) is something you are learning to get used to. As is the fact that she usually interrupts you, and often doesn't finish what she says, leaving you to guess what she is thinking.

Gill has another side which is darker and more troubling. Sometimes she becomes depressed and irritable, withdrawn and negative about the world and herself. She says she feels like committing suicide. It hurts you to see it. Then she goes off and takes drugs. You can't stay home all night or all day, and police her. You know soon enough when she's taken something. Her personality becomes extroverted and "over-the-top": hysterical laughter, talking non-stop, making no sense at times. After a few hours, her spirits sink, and she may end up depressed again, shouting, raging and smashing things. After that, she sleeps as if she were almost dead, and wakes up to give you floods of tears and apologies.

Gill once went to a party in her excited state (without you) and got in trouble with the police when they raided the premises and found drugs. You "gave it to her" afterwards, saying how you were ashamed of her. More hysterics followed. A few days later, and she's back to her usual happy, absent-minded, charming self.

Is she bipolar? There isn't any definite cycle: just random depression, and overexcited episodes followed by chaos, which occurs when she takes drugs. At times, you say Gillian catches dreams like hooking a great white shark, or else she sits there and catches nothing.

Your family doesn't like her. You wonder if you should ever have children together. When you think about breaking up, it makes you fear that she'd take her life if you did.

Finally, she agrees with you that she should try taking antidepressants. Your doctor thinks it's a possibility but wants an evaluation first. The psychiatric and psychological opinion comes: It's ADHD. Gillian should have different medication and you both would benefit from couples counseling. She's shocked and depressed. Does it mean she has a disease? Is she crazy? That's what people tell her sometimes – haven't you said, "That's crazy!" a million times over the two years you've been together?

You finally understand something you didn't before. Is life with her going to get any better, though?

There is hope. Someone like Gillian needs to come to terms with her condition, and you do as well. These two stories have been told here to give you an insight as to what ADHD might look like in a man and in a woman. It might not appear exactly this way in your relationship, but if your partner has ADHD, you should see something familiar there.

At the end of Chapter Three, I have included a brief questionnaire with things to ask yourself about your partner, and also things for your partner to ask himself or herself, if they have never had a diagnosis. These cannot take the place of a professional's detailed evaluation, but they may help you to seek one, or to realize that it's possible your partner has been living with ADHD since childhood.

I will explain to you exactly what ADHD is and what your partner has to live with. Then you will learn about some of the many problems sufferers get themselves into, and why. Further on, you will discover what techniques and skills you can both use to manage your life together. You can be happy, communicate and understand one another. If you are someone who's broken up a relationship, gone through a divorce, or been left by someone who has ADHD, this information can at least help you to understand why your experience was painful and what really happened. Whether you can or should go back to that person is something that can't be decided by me. However, sometimes knowing the truth can make it possible. If not, you can go on living with more peace: perhaps you'll know better how to handle that workmate, difficult member of your family, or anyone who is part of your life that might have ADHD. It isn't so rare.

PART 1 - UNDERSTANDING THE ADHD AND ITS IMPACT

CHAPTER 1: DEFINING ADHD: WHAT EXACTLY IS IT?

I am going to describe this problem to you as simply as I can. To be honest, some of the technical and psychologists' descriptions are very complicated, and can leave your head spinning. So I will sum it up for you, so you can have a basic idea of what causes your partner's problems.

At the same time, I want to make a few useful and often-forgotten observations to help you see what's most relevant to your relationship.

Attention Deficit/Hyperactivity Disorder (ADHD) is the name given to an imbalance which starts in the brain and nerves, and causes symptoms throughout life, which may worsen or improve with age. Restlessness, lack of concentration, problems with planning, controlling emotions with difficulty, or a habit of making snap, impulsive decisions are some of the most common behaviors a sufferer will experience.

Symptoms begin in childhood. People became very aware of this syndrome in the mid-to-late 20th century in little boys at school who were "hyperactive." As time goes by, we are realizing that some sufferers are not so obvious, especially the girls. While some people seem to learn about their weaknesses and control themselves better after adolescence, hiding their challenge quite effectively, the problem isn't something one just "grows out of." Conversely, some manage well in their younger years and begin to struggle when they hit the challenges of adulthood and independence.

ADD is more or less the same as ADHD. They used to call it ADD, and more recently the H for Hyperactivity was added because this is an important symptom for many people affected by this problem.

ADHD can be mild, moderate or severe. Some people have other behavioral challenges at the same time: they might suffer from depression or Asperger's Syndrome, to give two examples. However, they might be understood best as having ADHD, rather than being diagnosed with other conditions.

How common is this disorder? That depends on who you ask. The broadest view is that between 5 and 7 percent of children have some degree of ADHD. This is if a psychologist uses the

DSM-5 criteria, which refers to the Diagnostic and Statistical Manual (Fifth Edition) produced in the USA by the American Psychiatric Association. On the other hand, the ICD-10 criteria from the World Health Organization (the International Statistical Classification of Diseases and Related Health Problems, tenth edition) identify about 1 to 2 percent of children as sufferers. That's a more conservative view. We think about twice as many boys have ADHD as girls, though people used to believe it was very rare in females. Over the past thirty years, experts have come to see how wrong that was. The ratio of 2:1 males to females looks similar to the statistics for autism and related conditions.

In adults, you could be looking at a percentage of as much as 2 to 5 percent.

All right, what does this information mean?

Your loved one, if he or she knows about the diagnosis, is not making this up! It's definitely not all in the mind. You must understand that it is a physical problem that causes certain types of behavior. It's not deliberate, and isn't the result of making bad decisions or getting into bad habits. Someone may get into the pattern of shouting his head off whenever life gets him down, but taken on its own, that's probably something he's learnt to do. ADHD, however, is inborn and involuntary.

ADHD is not your average struggle to organize yourself on a bad day. The actual condition can be complicated to describe, and you might be dealing with one type of ADHD, or another. You partner might have ADHD and another neurological condition as well, or may turn out not to have classic ADHD at all, in the opinion of an expert...

Ouch! Take heart: the fact is that whatever it is exactly, the things you need to realize and the things you need to do are very similar. Think of these points:

- Your partner suffers from an undesired problem that both of you need to accept exists;

- He or she needs patience, communication and the right kind of help;

- The problem is lifelong, and can be helped in most cases by medicine and special counseling, but can't be cured;

- There is an excellent possibility that he or she can learn to handle it better, and live a happier, more intimate and more productive life with you.

Your reaction should take into account whatever the exact type of ADHD your partner has, but the guidelines in this book have a common core: love, acceptance, perseverance, communication and understanding.

ADHD seems to have a genetic origin, since it is statistically much more likely for a sufferer to have a brother or sister with the condition than it is for a non-sufferer. It's also possible that it could happen spontaneously as a genetic fault some time after conception, without being inherited. That's the same as with other genetic problems.

Scientists and medical experts have identified areas of the brain that seem to be under-developed in ADHD sufferers. Other areas may be more developed than usual, either because that's how the individual was born, or because the brain is trying to make up for deficiencies in other areas (like the strong arms of a wheelchair athlete). There is also a similarity between ADHD and childhood trauma victims, childhood accident victims with brain injury, and adults with post-traumatic shock symptoms. The parts of the brain affected are alike.

Please note that this does not imply that your loved one was mistreated as a child. Research has shown that most sufferers are from normally functioning families. When a child's emotional and relational upbringing is poor, it can affect their coping skills, but it is not the cause of their ADHD.

Psychiatrists know that something is happening to the nerve connections in the brain and nervous system of a person with

ADHD. Certain reactions and connections are too slow, or happen differently to the rest of us (whom they call "neurotypical"). The chemicals involved have been identified, and the effect is wide-ranging. Our knowledge of these chemicals, though still not complete, is what made the development of drugs to treat ADHD possible.

Other problems can occur together with ADHD. These may also be neurological, such as schizophrenia or autism of some kind, or they could be brain problems such as epilepsy. These are considered inborn problems. Other problems may be a result of an ADHD individual's behavior. Examples of these are alcoholism and drug abuse. People with ADHD might be strongly attracted to drugs because they offer relief from their symptoms, but drug use and alcohol overuse might cause further ADHD damage in the brain.

My advice is to be realistic; be aware that ADHD occur simultaneously with other problems. In the next chapter I go through the symptoms and signs of ADHD in more detail. However, don't jump to conclusions about drug abuse and alcohol being the root cause of your partner's problems, without evidence. They may not be involved at all.

Lastly, ADHD doesn't make people stupid, nor is it a sure sign of some eccentric professor. Its victims all battle a little harder with the average concentration and memory tests, but they range from seriously underdeveloped individuals who can't really live an independent life, through to people like you and me, all the way to exceptionally gifted geniuses. People who have ADHD are simply human beings – who happen to have ADHD.

CHAPTER 2: IDENTIFYING ADHD SYMPTOMS IN ADULTS

I n this chapter, we will look at the kinds of symptoms people with ADHD display. You will see that there are different types and presentations of ADHD, and understand some of the other problems are that can be encountered together with ADHD.

Yes, this involves classifications. Read this to help observe things your partner does, and identify conflicts and challenges in your relationship. You will likely see him or her in some but not all of the descriptions. You want to understand someone you love, so obviously you will be eager to know more.

However if you find yourself debating whether he or she is a "predominantly hyperactive type with oppositional defiant disorder", or a "combined hyperactive type with periodic inattentive episodes and denial of the condition"...don't fret about it!

If you know that your partner has ADHD, whatever the presentation, leave the diagnosis to a professional. All you need to do at first is accept that your partner has this challenge, and he or she needs to accept the truth without shame. Then you can start working on yourself to become more understanding, and learn the best and most effective ways to help and communicate with your partner. There are wrong ways to try to help, and I will explain why this is so, and what the best methods are.

One crucial key to understanding ADHD and its effects, is that it interferes with the brain's ability to organize. We all need to switch between thoughts and impressions, make decisions, decide what is more important and what is less. At the root of all the ADHD symptoms are problems with doing just these things.

As we know, symptoms begin in childhood. However, some people don't show them in childhood as clearly as others. Moreover, as one grows older, the symptoms change and are presented somewhat differently. There are three basic types of ADHD, which can look different during childhood and adulthood.

1) The Predominantly Inattentive Presentation of ADHD

When young, this person is "The Dreamer." The boy who looks out of the window or just seems to be somewhere else at times. These people will omit details, misunderstand instructions at home or school, and find concentrating difficult. They'll forget things or lose them, and often be shouted at because they don't seem to be paying attention when being spoken to (which, many times, they're not...) and usually avoid doing things that require continuous mental effort.

A child in school might rush to put up his hand when the teacher asks for the names of some marine animals. His classmate is chosen, and says, "A whale." Then he is chosen, and says, "I... sorry, I forgot." He was going to say, "A seal" when he raised his hand, but in the tiny little tense moment of being chosen by the teacher, he went blank. His teacher will be irritated if he doesn't suspect ADHD, and his classmates roll their eyes.

To be classified, a person must consult a qualified professional. Most guidelines agree that the signs of ADHD should have appeared between the ages of six and twelve, and must have lasted longer than six months. They should manifest themselves in several situations, such as in the family, at school or work; and they should be severe enough to classify the individual as having problems with daily interaction.

As an adult, this condition may be harder to recognize. Everyone learns coping skills and workarounds on the path to adulthood.

Perhaps she seems slightly blank when you have a longer conversation with her, but she carries on looking at you and nodding her head, saying, "I see." Actually, halfway through your telling her about what happened, she lost the thread of what you were saying, and tried bravely to carry on listening to you while she racked her brain to remind herself what it was all about. Then you see her suddenly light up, almost jump, and she looks more attentive. That's because she remembered what it you were talking about. She is hiding this from herself as much as from you, because she doesn't know any other way to experience listening to a longer conversation. It's been like this all her life. If you didn't understand ADHD, you would likely be confused and slightly irritated.

The room or house lived in by such an ADHD sufferer will be cluttered and disorganised. This is probably going to be the case for all of the three presentations.

2) The Predominantly Hyperactive-Impulsive Presentation of ADHD

This sufferer will be "The Fidgeter" at school and at dinner time. He will never sit still, and will notice everything going on around him, from the classmate who drops her book, to the airplane flying overhead, to the coin in his pocket that he takes out compulsively, everything – except the task at hand. He has much more physical and mental energy than the first type, all of it being his worst enemy, as it leads to him being completely unfocused. Younger ones run around endlessly, make a lot of noise, and cannot stand waiting. They are known to burst out with an answer before the person who's asking has finished the question, to jump queues, and to play out of turn in games. They also struggle to listen to instructions or conversations, interrupt other people, and may talk very fast without giving others a chance to take part in the conversation.

An adult might not run around at work, but he might play endlessly with his pen, using it as a drumstick. He may be impulsive, getting sudden inspiration and ideas, but will often not finish what he began. He might drive around in his free time, trying to help his family or friends, but leave things undone at home. If you are his wife or girlfriend, you'd find this hurtful and really exhausting. You might battle to keep up with what he's doing, and just want him to spend more time with you. When you tell him this, he seems apologetic, but then offers to take you out to do something when you are tired. He just doesn't seem to want to spend time at home. You seem to spend half your life reminding him not to forget things, or helping him to find them... Little wonder that you become angry, frustrated, or call him selfish and crazy. Knowing that it's ADHD won't immediately solve his problems with organizing his life, but it might save you a lot of frustration, doubts about his motives, and even stop you from wondering if he still loves you.

All people with ADHD may become very angry and frustrated with themselves, but especially those with this second presentation. Their impatience, in more outgoing or assertive personalities, can turn into losing their temper, and venting their frustration and feelings of being out of control. Physical exertion can be very beneficial to hyperactive victims of ADHD, but I have to add that, when they're living undiagnosed, this could turn into an obsession. Have you ever known a compulsive runner who spends all his free time out practicing for marathons, and can't talk about anything else? That might be a sign of a related condition such as Asperger's Syndrome, but when the victim is always restless, always impatient and can't concentrate on other tasks, it looks more like ADHD. It could be both. As we know, sufferers of ADHD can have other psychological, brain-related problems at the same time.

3) The Combined Type Presentation of ADHD

This is a combination of the first two types, where an individual acts in both manners at different times, or even in the same moment. Such a person would seem to be "The Stop-and-Go." There might be a tendency for adults, especially when older, to have started out as Hyperactive-Impulsives, and mellowed into more typical Inattentive types by their twenties, thirties or forties.

Now I have covered the three classifications of ADHD sufferers. Some experts prefer to just put them all on a continuum, a sliding scale from one extreme to the other.

An important bit of advice to give here, when dealing with adults, is that you will gain a lot of understanding of your partner if you knew what he or she was like as a child, especially if you suspect ADHD, or know it, but don't understand what type it is. Your partner's family and childhood friends will be able to give you some useful information. I must leave it to you as to whether asking them yourself would be the most respectful or loving thing to do. Perhaps your partner will be willing to do it himself or herself, or the two of you could talk to their parents together.

This isn't meant to imply that your partner is incapable of telling you anything directly. Rather, an ADHD sufferer may not have remembered well what things were like for them as a child, or was unable to realize at the time what was happening. Also, no-one relishes the memory of being humiliated in front of other classmates, or shouted at for misunderstanding the rules of sport, for example, and they might push this memory away. It's very hard to comprehend how other people saw you and experienced your actions, if you have ADHD. Standing in other people's shoes isn't easy for any of us, and it's harder still for them. Sufferers may gain great insight into others' perspectives as they grow older – but obviously that wasn't the case when they were younger. Though some people with this disorder go on to have very good long-term memories, this condition can affect recall, memory, and organization. It follows that they may have taken longer to form clear memories of their childhood than non-sufferers usually do.

What other things characterize an ADHD sufferer, that you need to understand? I must mention their lack of concentration – especially sustained concentration. This is really odd to a non-sufferer, and is often the cause of much misunderstanding.

A boy or girl might have a fascination with a certain sport, or animals, for example. This topic will hold their attention so tightly that they become fixated on it. They will often excel in this area, and give it all the concentration it needs. This could also be an abstract or highly-specialized skill, such as mathematics or astronomy. At the same time (and do remember what I said about ADHD sufferers not necessarily being geniuses), they will perform badly at other tasks, recall other areas of knowledge poorly, and find abstract thinking (not connected to their hobby or obsession) very hard.

This explanation of ADHD assumes that you love and want the best for your partner, whatever state your relationship is in, or even if it's ended. You want to understand what goes on in their head, and you are willing to assume the best reason or motive for their actions. Unfortunately, many people aren't so well-disposed. Seeing this contradictory problem with attention – too little or too much – they assume the ADHD sufferer is selfish and arrogant, obsessed only with themselves and things he or she cares about.

What effect is ADHD having here? It makes concentration on the routine, the everyday, the difficult, excruciatingly laborious work. One might object and say, "Don't all of us have to put in a bit of effort to do our work every day? Who doesn't find getting up in the morning an effort?" But we fail to realize that we can and do manage to do boring, repetitive, or abstract tasks quite successfully, without half-killing ourselves. The ADHD sufferer, as his or her brain-scan might just show, is straining frantically from childhood, in an ongoing effort to make sense of a world full of "white noise." The effort needed is far greater because organizing is so much more difficult for them.

This can lead to childhood trauma and damage. People with this disorder are often punished and scolded for "not trying hard enough," even, in the case perhaps of the inattentive type, called "lazy." It pays to think about the answers most of them give when asked how they manage to concentrate so well on their pet subjects. They usually say something like, "But this is so easy. It just makes sense." I believe such words as these need to be accepted and understood. They are saying that their reason for being fascinated by postage stamps, ice-hockey, sci-fi literature, nuclear physics, or whatever, is that they find it easy to concentrate on! They seem to have an inborn "feel" for animals, or colors and textures, certain ideas, or certain movements, for example. Does this have anything to do with what scientists are discovering about the brains of people with neurological problems such as ADHD? That they are underdeveloped in some areas, but extremely well developed in other ways? I believe this merits further consideration, in order to understand them better.

My point is that for this reason it is horribly unfair to think your partner is bored with you, and cares only about his or her fortés, hobbies and obsessions. I know that won't make a person with ADHD easy for you to live with. It will be tiring. But just stand in his or her shoes, and think about how tiring life can be for your partner.

Another symptom of ADHD is the occasional ability to make clever or extremely subtle observations, and then perhaps also memorize them for years. They might also remember odd and out-of-context facts. This begins in childhood. It's both a blessing and a curse.

Because most sufferers find social conventions and assumptions rather difficult to grasp, they may be able to think and act without prejudice or carelessness, on occasions. They aren't likely to be blinded by "Oh, everyone knows we all do such-and-such" thinking. For example, this could lead a teenager to see, observe and identify criminal activity in her neighborhood because it looks out of place, in a situation where nobody else bothers to look at things. A boy might find a fossil in an old quarry, saying that its unusual form just stood out for him. Everyone else there just sees stone. Sufferers of ADHD may become accepting and unsnobbish adults who take people as they find them, without rejecting eccentrics or "outsiders." They may be quite good at seeing bad motives and avoiding manipulative people because there are little "giveaways" and warning signs.

Conversely, ADHD sufferers may become rigidly prejudiced, clinging to ideas they grew up with, to give them security. They could become bigoted and intolerant, because it is harder for them to understand others. They may miss really obvious social clues, and end up being deceived and used by manipulative individuals, because they took them at face value.

Your partner might be able to make funny and brilliant remarks or observations – at least, sometimes. Certain people might see this as evidence of a genius. They may say so to others. Un-knowingly, that puts a huge strain of others' presumption onto the ADHD sufferer. Now people meet him or her, expecting a genius. They may be disappointed. A different, less charitable person sees these remarks alongside the ADHD sufferer's mis-takes and apparent foolishness, and thinks your partner is a liar who is ignorant or forgetful. Uncharitable people tend to share their opinions. "He said he knew what cryptocurrency is. Then he talked about the 'Australian pound', and we corrected him. He just said, 'Sorry, dollar.' Do you really believe that he can 'forget' that currency?" Now people meet your partner, expecting a con-artist. Or else, such unloving people ignore what your partner does know and can do, and treat them like a fool.

Underneath all this is a human being with strengths and weaknesses, as we all are. There's just a marked and unusual pattern about them. Once you see that, you can understand your ADHD partner better. There might be a lot of hurt and anger lingering there, I must add.

In order to make a diagnosis, a psychologist needs to judge that someone's symptoms are severe enough to make everyday life difficult. He or she will be trained to identify, interview and evaluate them, to see through the thinking of some family members or associates who say, "But doesn't everyone forget sometimes?" or, "Don't we all fidget in our seats if we've been driving for hours?" The person with ADHD may cling to this kind of thinking, probably drilled into him or her from childhood. They may try to laugh it off, or feel offended by the suggestion that they have a "condition" or "mental illness."

A good evaluation and treatment of ADHD needs to involve you, the sufferer's partner. You might be the one to notice improvements, or see telling signs of his or her problems with organizing the brain.

I want to now deal further with some of the related problems I mentioned in Chapter One that can be caused by, aggravated by, or just occur together with ADHD.

General depression, bipolar disorder, anxiety disorder, learning problems such as dyslexia, milder autism disorders or borderline schizophrenia, personality disorders, substance abuse, reactions to medication, accident trauma and brain damage, and even dementia can produce symptoms similar to ADHD. That must sound awful to you, someone who is in a romantic relationship with a sufferer of ADHD. Lists of symptoms in medical manuals are always depressing reading, especially for laypeople who just want to understand the world of mental health a little better.

What this is saying is that maybe there is something else troubling your partner, or possibly even that one of these is the root cause of the problem. Diagnosing this is the specialty of medical professionals. Leaving them to their part in helping your partner, it is better to think of an example of three well-known diseases to show you how symptoms of different disorders can be very similar, or quite different.

Take the common cold, influenza and the now-infamous Covid-19.

All three of these are respiratory infections. There's no rule to say that you can't suffer from more than one at a time, but that's not the most common presentation. A cold is usually less severe, and fever is more common with the latter two. All of them can cause coughs, but Covid-19 can cause a dry cough with difficulty breathing. Colds and influenza can make you sneeze and throw out large quantities of mucus, Covid-19 can cause sneezing but mucus is not produced so copiously. Colds can make you feel as if you want to rest, influenza can make you feel really tired, and Covid-19 might make you totally exhausted. However, there's a lot of overlap, and sometimes you just don't know what you have, especially at the beginning. Call the doctor!

The basic treatment is very similar in all cases; hygiene such as washing your hands, disposing of paper handkerchiefs, resting, avoiding contact with other people, hydration and some analgesic medicine.

Similarly, what you must do as the non-ADHD partner in a relationship is more or less the same, whatever the exact type of ADHD he or she suffers, or even when other conditions are present. Understand, accept, communicate, and know when to step in, and when not to.

ADHD victims can also fall into maladaptive and problematic behaviors. Yes, neurotypical people can also behave in these ways, but ADHD sufferers have a greater likelihood of displaying these problems.

Dangers include a greater risk of accidents in childhood, often continuing into adulthood. The reason for this seems to be because some individuals have poor co-ordination. They would have been clumsy as kids, perhaps learning to walk later than other toddlers, have done badly at sport, and had many problems with handwriting or using keyboards. As adults one can imagine them slipping and falling more often, or having small accidents when driving. Of course, they might have good or even above-average co-ordination, but have accidents caused by poor concentration instead... or they might have both problems! This is the frustrating nature of neurological conditions: often they don't affect any two individuals in the same way.

Hyperactive-impulsive ADHD sufferers are probably at a higher risk of accidents because of poor concentration, and rapid, uncontrolled movements. One can see how this might throw you off a bicycle as a boy, and later make you slam your foot on the brake as a man (when all you should have done was slow down). So many of our daily activities call for quick but accurate judgements – crossing a street, for example. Is your partner the one who launches herself into the street before an oncoming car because she's late for work, and has to run to get out of the way?

Life with ADHD can be depressing. Sufferers have a higher rate of depression than neurotypicals (non-sufferers), and are also more likely to try to medicate or alleviate their feelings with substances. Alcohol can often become an escape, but since it is a calming agent, ADHD sufferers tend to use stimulants more. Some people drink coffee frantically. While many of us say, "But I can't start the day without it!" ADHD sufferers' use of coffee (and the resulting hyperactivity) is in often a class of its own. If you drink six a day, they'll be drinking twenty, perhaps!

Chocolate also contains caffeine, as well as other substances that sufferers crave. "Huh!" I can hear some people saying, "I can't eat half a bar of chocolate. I must eat all of it. What's the difference?" Again, it's a case of degree and severity. Can you really not stop yourself from getting up at night on Easter Saturday and eating ALL your children's Easter eggs that you wrapped specially for them? More specifically, the last time you ate chocolate, what happened? Did you start feeling a sort of buzzing "high," your hands shook, your heart pounded, but you felt... wonderful?

Do you rush to the coffee machine at the first break, pushing in front of other colleagues to flick the handle of the dispenser with trembling hands, and then run to the kettle? It's been one-and-a-half hours since your last cup! You yourself probably don't behave this way, but if your partner treats caffeine like this, and has an ADHD diagnosis, you will understand that there's a likely connection.

Stimulants don't end there; they include cocaine, amphetamines manufactured illegally, and so many more hard drugs" It is more likely for ADHD sufferers to end up abusing them.

Stimulants aid them in organizing their brains and concentrating, giving them a relief they can feel. In fact, medications used to treat ADHD are often carefully-designed stimulants; but illegal drugs can provide a kind of relief that turns into a kaleidoscope of excited confusion, or fear and anger, even psychosis – and they can become violently addictive.

More ADHD people are smokers than neurotypicals, and they tend to smoke more than neurotypical smokers, on average. An interesting and maybe very important little fact is that sometimes ADHD makes people react differently (or even in the opposite way) than expected when taking medicines, drugs and other mind-altering chemicals. To continue with the example of caffeine: your loved one might be one of those people who can eat a large bar of chocolate, drink a couple of black coffees, take an aspirin for back pain, and start falling asleep at the kitchen table before going to bed and sleeping for several hours. Similarly, the tranquilizer you get when a doctor puts an endoscope down your throat to look at your stomach might have very little relaxing effect on your partner. He might panic and vomit during the procedure, and afterwards be tapping his feet with impatience instead of resting. The cup of tea the nurse offers will go down in one gulp, and when it is time to lead the patient to the car to be driven home, the supposedly wobbly, sleepy person will jump up and run, literally pulling the nurse behind him. Something in the brain structure and chemical balance of an ADHD sufferer lies behind this occasional symptom. It's worthwhile asking your partner if anything like this has ever happened. If so, it's a good idea to tell their doctor, and any medical professional who does an evaluation for ADHD.

Handling emotions with ADHD is more difficult than for most people. Part of our handling emotions consists of balancing different feelings and various knowledge – e.g. my desire to retaliate to an insult; my thoughts that my insulter is a foreign-language speaker who doesn't understand that the word he used was much stronger than it is in his native tongue; my awareness of my family who are with me and trying to back me up, and who are also trying to calm me down. In a situation like this, if one had ADHD it may all prove to be too much to handle, provoking a complete rage, punching the aggressor, and so on.

Other problematic behaviors include risk-taking activities we do for thrills, like driving rally cars or going mountain climbing. An ADHD-affected person might not feel or realize the danger of hurtling down a mountain pass with sharp bends, as he drives in his car. It is as if he sees the town at the foot of the mountain and just starts driving towards it in his mind, without the awareness of the hairpin bends on the way down.

Sport can be a relaxing and beneficial activity for someone with ADHD, and more of that will be said later. However, the addictive behavior I am dealing with here is the rush of adrenaline that can easily become excessive and dangerous. Dangerous challenges are interesting to look at from the point of view of the sufferer. While you might be tearing out your hair seeing your loved one putting his or her life at risk, he or she is doing something that causes intense concentration. Concentration is the very thing he or she struggles to do, and whatever achieves it, is seen as extremely pleasant. Danger concentrates your mind powerfully, to misquote Dr Samuel Johnson. Danger is danger for everyone, but given that ADHD affects concentration, memory and decision-making, it makes sufferers more likely to make mistakes, in situations where mistakes have greater consequences.

Greater incidences of violent behavior, anti-social attitudes stemming from feelings of rejection, and poorer health from substance abuse, junk food, or sheer forgetfulness with regard to healthy diet and regular exercise, all mark the lives of some sufferers. Most of them sleep badly and irregularly. Some can't fall asleep till late, then can't wake up. Others simply don't sleep well; and yet others sleep as if they were cats.

In order to help your partner, you must try and get into his or her shoes. Think about what it's like to grow up with a "noise in your head," as some sufferers describe it, and live in a world that never seems to be in sync with you. Everything distracts you; even enjoyable activities leave your head spinning – or perhaps you just disappear into the inner world of your daydreams, where you can arrange everything so much more clearly and enjoy your favourite thoughts and memories. Your childhood was full of endless corrections, slapped wrists, pulled reins, and the words, "Shut up!" Sitting at table for a light meal was like hearing an Icelandic saga over several days, and being in class at school was mostly a wait for break time.

What about conversations? Imagine that whenever you made a comment, you were told not to interrupt, or laughed because what you said always seemed to come from somewhere else. Deciding to shut up, as you were told, you kept quiet until your mental dam burst, when you then talked non-stop till you were silenced again. Maybe you rebelled and said what you wanted to say, to cheek them, or just because you could. You used words as weapons to defend yourself from all the criticism you'd put up with.

Imagine you knew things most other children in class didn't know, but failed to memorize your times table, or used the wrong word in a sentence. You heard your teacher say, "You can't tell me you don't know that. Last week you got nine out of ten. What's wrong with you?" Worse still, you might read words on your report card such as, "She's perfectly good at History, but seems not to want to make an effort," when you know you were trying. Once you are an adult, you realize, with deep anger and shame, that you were actually trying harder than just about anyone else there. Trying to make sense of your surroundings was what you were doing from day one.

Add to this what it must be like to have few friends; perhaps to love intensely the few you have, and for your world to crash whenever they disagree with you, or you make them angry. When daytime life is a space between cigarettes, a wild escape from nagging people and endless, depressing, panic-inducing deadlines that you never seem to make, or that your long practice of last-minute rushing has helped you become accustomed to.

Hopefully, you might be getting some new insights now into the mind of your partner. This is not to put any blame on you if you find your relationship has been exhausting and stressful, and it's also not an excuse for any of his or her bad, or at least harmful, behavior. People with ADHD need to learn how to handle themselves in the right way.

Instead, this was a detailed overview of what Attention-Deficit/Hyperactivity Disorder looks like in the lives of those people it affects. In the following chapters, we will go into some specific aspects of ADHD, and examine particular types of sufferers and certain situations that are likely to arise.

CHAPTER 3: HOW DOES ADHD MANIFEST DIFFERENTLY IN WOMEN COMPARED TO MEN?

I t can be a little bit depressing to read the polarized opinions about men and women put out in the media. Sometimes it seems that men really are from Mars, and women are from planet Zorg...

If you are the male partner of a woman who has an ADHD diagnosis, it's quite likely that she hasn't known about it for very long. Many more women than men live undiagnosed. Often their symptoms aren't seen for what they truly are, or are hidden by adult coping mechanisms that don't really heal or improve their problems. If you are the female partner of a man with ADHD, it is still worthwhile for you to compare his challenges with those of a woman in his situation.

This chapter is also going to deal with the way people with ADHD experience dating, long-term relationships and marriage, contrasting women with men in areas where it applies. Some readers who may still be unsure about whether their spouse suffers from ADHD or not will find help at the end. There you will find a questionnaire which you and your partner can answer to help you both to get an idea of whether she or he really does have ADHD. You can't tell for sure without a professional diagnosis, but it can act as a helpful guide.

For readers who are in a relationship with a partner of the same sex, this book is also relevant. Any relationship, and even friendship, requires two people to understand and co-operate with each other, a balance that ADHD makes difficult to achieve, especially when it isn't known about or understood. I could add my belief here that there would be both advantages and disadvantages when two male or two female brains, with their unique thought processes and emotions, have a close bond. In some cases a woman will see more easily what another woman sees, even though one has ADHD and the other doesn't. Likewise, two men can see life from a male point of view, and they wouldn't need to wonder if misunderstandings were simply a matter of gender. However, two similar minds without the benefit of a different outlook might intensify their communication problems if the effects of ADHD are not recognized. It all comes down to understanding what ADHD is, accepting it as a challenge, and working together to find ways around its obstacles to happy communication.

We know about the differences in biology and brain structure between men and women, and so we might expect differences in behavior between men and women with ADHD. We do see this, and I believe society plays a part in this.

When they're young, boys and girls with ADHD don't present it in the same way, and girls don't show it as clearly. Until we have some sort of yes-or-no biological test for ADHD, researchers can't always know who they are missing, or whom they mistakenly diagnose with it. It's also important to say that girls were diagnosed very rarely until the 1970s, when psychology woke up to the fact that this condition does affect females. Now, with ADHD diagnoses among boys being so high in the US and other western countries that the medical profession and educators risk over-diagnosing it, the percentage of girls has risen to about 40 to 45 percent of the number of boys diagnosed. This tells us that, in the past, girls certainly went undiagnosed far more often, and probably still are missed more frequently. Those girls who were undiagnosed in the past are now women of all ages.

The partner of a woman with ADHD might very well by shocked to hear her diagnosis. They may associated this condi-tion as "hyperactivity" in little boys? But you can see from the previous chapter that ADHD varies in its symptoms.

Females are more often seen to have the Inattentive type of ADHD, or the Combined, than males. Their brain organiza-tion isn't as badly affected with regard to physical, dimension-al movements. However, just because girls aren't as likely to be climbing lamp posts at break time, this doesn't mean they aren't struggling with ADHD. The Inattentive-type male is also overlooked more often, but not handled with such impatience. Adults often tolerate boys losing attention more than we do girls, and girls' social and language skills frequently being more fluent than boys', we expect that girls will pay attention to what we say, and that they'll understand it.

We think of average and above-average women multi-tasking at work and home. Somehow, subtly, it becomes expected of them. A woman must be able to cook, talk to the relative who is helping her, answer the questions of her daughter who doesn't understand her homework, and answer the phone – all at the same time.

As we know, ADHD is actually an organizing problem, deep down in the brain. A female suffering from this disorder is simply not going to be able to divide her attention as well as a neurotypical woman does. When she can't, not only does she have to tackle the disappointed expectations, but she has to make quick decisions which are extremely traumatic for her. She will feel overwhelmed and anxious; these two feelings can become dominant.

Physical exercise can have a beneficial effect on those with this disorder, and any movement seems to help sufferers to relax physically, if not concentrate. Especially in adult female ADHD sufferers, the restlessness seems to become internalized, and an outward dreamer may be frightened, overwhelmed and tense on the inside, not really showing it in a casual interaction.

"I'm overwhelmed" or, "It's all too much for me right now," are expressions that often describe the way a typical female ADHD sufferer feels inside. I believe this holds true whether or not she is at the Inattentive end of the scale, or the Hyperactive and Impulsive end, or somewhere in between. She might avoid crowded social events or noisy environments, saying that they make her head spin. Then she might just go off to a pop concert with one friend, saying, "I don't mind it because I can concentrate on the music, and my friend and I aren't having a conversation." She will probably also have cotton wool in her ears to keep the noise down slightly. Sensitivity to noise seems to be a feature of ADHD and several other neurological conditions, though not in all cases. In this case of a pop concert, there isn't a variety of things to concentrate on; there's just one, really, when you are in the arena and listening. Of course, one does have to get there...

Being punctual is a huge challenge for many ADHD sufferers, and being tidy, another. Life can progress differently for them in this aspect, and may differ between males and females. Young boys may visibly, physically disorder their surroundings, while young girls tend to leave things as they are. On the inside, both are battling to find their way around, and to remember positions, and above all, sequences. An apparently tidier girl is often hiding a deep inner stress from losing awareness of and not being able to regulate the things and people who surround her. I used the word "sequences" deliberately. ADHD can leave an individual's memory for small facts and his or her powers of observation unaffected – but their short-term memory and ability to order one memory after another will often be bad.

For example: what do you do when you are preparing to leave your house? First, you put on all your outer clothes except your hat. Then you get your larger handbag and the plastic bags you are going to re-use, and put the plastic bags in a pocket of your coat. You get the keys to the house and put them in your bag. You make sure you have your bus ticket in the purse, and that the purse is in the outer pocket of the handbag. Then you get your hat and put it on, and walk out of the door, which will lock behind you as you pull it closed. Now you can walk out of the gate and off to the bus stop. That's an imaginary example.

It's a sequence of individual things and actions. On the bus, you suddenly recall: I never brought the shopping list! There will be another sequence of actions for returning home.

All of us do things like this: rows of memorized, routine actions. Our order of events is probably stable and almost automatic, but can be adapted with an effort that isn't too stressful. The shopping list probably should have come after your purse, or just before it. It can happen that we leave something out. An ADHD-affected person may try to stick rigidly to the same order, but even then, one step will just fail to materialize. It could be any one: the keys, the plastic bags, the hat, even the handbag. Other affected people never achieve any workable order and do things in a different sequence each time! This can make life very difficult.

All of this effort to focus makes an Inattentive type tired. It's simply easier to stop the mental effort for a few seconds to get some energy back. The stress is unpleasant, felt very powerfully, and can lead to depression.

Some male ADHD sufferers adopt what looks like a carefree attitude, maybe saying something like, "I'll make a plan to get into the house when I get back there," or, "I'll just buy the stuff I can remember. The rest will have to wait for next time." But deep down, he's likely to be under stress as well. Yet because he's male, people will make more allowances for him. They aren't overly surprised when he returns from a shop with only one of the two items he was asked to buy. They may even admire his seemingly carefree outlook, saying that he may be a scatterbrain, but at least he is positive. Girls and women usually fail to get this kind of acceptance, and other women are frequently the ones to judge them harshly: "What do you mean, you 'forgot'? Don't you make a shopping list? Oh. You did, but you forgot to take it? That's pathetic!"

Some victims whose ADHD isn't severe may improve a lot once they become adults. They will have found ways to organize, by trial and error. Others actually have it worse once they leave home and school – women may be more likely to experience this. Life is generally simpler when you are a child, as deeply as any of us may suffer with our problems in youth. A caring home and school environment basically plans things with you and for you. Once you meet adult situations, and you have left home, you are alone. Perhaps you're studying, but college and university are places where you have to organize your own study. Or now you are working, and maybe married. You are expected to help other people to be organized. Undiagnosed ADHD probably is a case of something like this – having a good environment that supported you until you lost it later in life. This will be deeply stressful to a woman who was used to having some order in her life, and who thought her inner struggles were the same as anyone else's, who now finds herself criticized by a husband or boyfriend, or colleagues.

Over and over again, sufferers recall being criticized all through life, from an early age until the present. Sympathy is often denied. If she says she hates it when her supervisor at work stands over her and talks to her while she's on a phone call with a customer, she will likely hear her colleague say, "Well, just concentrate on the customer a bit more and say, 'Yes' every few seconds to keep him happy. I don't find doing that too difficult. Can't you just do something like that?"

A girl with ADHD may actually be a Hyperactive/Impulsive type, however school psychologists and parents may still not detect the source of her problems. She can be hyperactive, but it's probably going to manifest in extreme talkativeness and rapid emotional changes. It's important to say that her talkativeness is less the sign of a happy and extroverted person, and more the sign of a nervous and tense personality. Also, she might change subjects rapidly, not finish what she begins saying, and have difficulty pronouncing some words or combinations of words. Her constant talking and rapid changes of emotions may lead people to call her "rebellious" or "individualistic." She is less likely to make friends than her male counterparts: other girls may find her style of communicating odd and call her "selfish" for saying so much without being able to listen for the same length of time.

I believe any woman who has problems saying some words, and struggles to concentrate on written questions, deserves attention. ADHD sufferers are dyslexic more often than neurotypicals. They often do well in oral tests, yet find written instructions to be much less intelligible.

Emotions are things we all learn to handle, with a lot of mistakes on the way. A Hyperactive/Impulsive girl will have a terrible battle here. She is expected to feel her emotions, perhaps less criticized than a boy for showing them, but they must be expressed in the right way. She will be judged severely if she doesn't understand or guess what other people's emotional displays mean. ADHD sufferers often explode when the stress of dividing their attention becomes excessive, or react with an outburst of joy or sorrow they tend to express first, then try to control later.

A more extroverted victim who is impulsive and who hasn't been diagnosed sometimes turns into a would-be organizer who tries to do for others what she fails to achieve herself. She can become very frustrating for others, insisting on what they should wear, where they can buy the best ingredients, what the best restaurant is, how to feed their puppy... In the meantime, she keeps on starting new projects, but never seems to finish them; her house looks like a bomb site, and her non-stop opinions of how you could do things better cause some people to lose their temper. Why is this victim of ADHD doing this? To see the world as she does, you have to understand that the world looks noisy and confusing to her. The same people who become angry with her will often admit that she seems to mean well. She's trying to help, not from a desire to criticize you as such. Next, you must understand that her own confusion, her own mess, is depressing, as much and probably more for her as it is for someone else. From that standpoint, others' needs and even problems – yours, especially, if you are her partner – look simpler and easier to manage than her own. Unconsciously, this woman is trying to step back from her own tangle of organizing, by organizing someone else's life instead.

A male extrovert with ADHD may get some acceptance from his mother, other women, and perhaps you, his wife or part- ner. However, some men become talkative but conflictive, in a similar but more intense way to impulsive, restless women with ADHD. Finding their emotions hard to hold down, they can start arguments and even fights – as they tactlessly say what they think. It is entirely likely that all the criticism they have received in their lives will egg them on to be critical of others, apparently for the enjoyment of arguing. This is not to excuse the man who picks a fight, or the woman who airs her opinions loudly in defiance of another, or starts a screaming match. Many of these are probably not sufferers of ADHD. But I believe you will see in those ADHD sufferers who do these types of things, a tense, unhappy, depressed person who feels driven to lash out at what he or she sees as wrong – someone who doesn't enjoy arguing.

That isn't going to be easy to live with in the long term, especially if no-one knows what is really affecting her, or him. Once the problem is identified and there are guidelines for both partners to follow, it will be possible to live a happier and more peaceful life together.

How Sufferers of ADHD Struggle in Later Life and Adult Relationships

One of the most common results in female sufferers (and not a few men) is depression. The statistics speak volumes: over twice as many women with ADHD try to commit suicide compared to neurotypical women; they suffer perhaps three times the rate of depression.

It isn't merely the effort of trying to keep on top of life's demands that causes depression in women with ADHD. They have been shown to blame themselves significantly more than men do. Low self-esteem may make a male ADHD personality avoid and dismiss the challenges of his life. ("That's a whole lot of gobbledygook for me. I just don't go there.") Meanwhile, a female sufferer, more often undiagnosed, is prone to blaming herself for the negative feedback she hears. Being late, getting bad marks for assignments, a feeling of not even having a handle on the basic skills for life, makes her think she's stupid. Then along come the opinions of outsiders – she is selfish, immature, slightly crazy, or even just lazy!

Many societies have strong social pressures which demand that women should always apologize. ADHD makes this aggravatedly unpleasant, because a victim finds it proportionally harder to know if a mistake or omission was really her fault. It can be easier to assume it is, and thus begin a lifelong bad habit.

Women are statistically more likely to approach a counsellor or doctor for help. Unfortunately, because ADHD isn't always easy to diagnose, especially not from a short appointment, they may be told they suffer from depression, or a mood or anxiety disorder. Here's the tragedy: in addition to ADHD, these victims truly will be suffering from depression, anxiety , or a number of other psychological conditions. They may engage in self-harming behaviors such as cutting themselves, starving themselves, or otherwise acting out of deep feelings of self-hate.

Yet these diagnoses may do little to help. The reasons for these conditions only become apparent if ADHD is suspected or proved. Otherwise it's just a whole range of diverse problems throughout life that the expert may not be able to grasp.

Medication is a subject that must be covered, and more will be explained later. However, what can happen is that an anti-depressant will be ineffective, or it may have unwanted side-effects that make living with ADHD even worse. There is no one-size-fits-all medicine for neurological problems. Until the ADHD is treated with ADHD-specific medication, it may not help. ADHD victims are also known to react differently than expected to some stimulants, foods and medications.

One can only imagine the disappointment, sense of failure and shame that a woman with ADHD must experience when she has admitted that she needs help; then she's diagnosed with depression, had counselling and is taking antidepressants – and still doesn't feel any better at managing her daily life and work.

Acknowledging that people with ADHD have all sorts of different personalities (after all, someone with ADHD is simply a human being), there is one big problem for them when it comes to relationships. The so-called "honeymoon effect." Once more I find myself answering almost defensively to the question, "Doesn't every couple have to deal with this effect, and carry on once it's worn off?"

Yes, but not quite in the way it occurs when one partner has ADHD. The secret here is to recognize how ADHD affects someone in so many, subtle ways. It can look like other issues, or not even be noticed by the partner at first. The tendency of an ADHD-affected mind to hyper-focus makes victims seem very different at first, to the way they become when life has gone back to the post-honeymoon "normal."

You may have met your future partner and at once seen his or her virtues and good. If he, or especially she, was an Inattentive type then your very novelty as a new interest helped the ADHD sufferer pay attention to you. As an adult, a woman may, as I noted earlier, be able to hide the fact that she is losing the thread of your conversation. If she was unable to remember something you said because she didn't understand it, at first the non-ADHD boyfriend will be very understanding. Everyone strives to remember facts about new people. Similarly, women may see an inattentive ADHD man as a quiet and calm person, unaware of the fear, tiredness and anger he may hide while it looks like he's daydreaming.

Anybody feeling the sensations of being in love wants to pass over the defects of their partner. A man might say to himself about his ADHD girlfriend, "We'll make a plan to get her more social confidence." A woman may say of her ADHD boyfriend, "I'll fix him. I'll help him." Sometimes we dream about who our beloved can become, rather than loving who he or she really is. So even when they do tell you they have something called ADHD, and what it means, some people don't prepare themselves to look at the real challenges they are going to face. They think it's something they can ignore.

Hyperactive types can be exciting and interesting people. Their conversation may center on their interests, on which they can focus, or it may be quite broad. If the conversation is interesting, you might think about what they say and not bother too much that you don't get enough opportunities to reply or comment. Perhaps you are an assertive type who can make a break in a conversation without causing upset. Perhaps you aren't, but you just decide to be patient. If they speak of their hopes and projects, an ADHD partner can be inspiring and interesting, when it's all new.

The features of hyper-focusing mean, first of all, that when YOU are the center of their attention, you will get lots of it. Obviously they aren't just making the effort in order to deceive you. It's genuine. What can happen to the hyper-focus, though? It can wear off. More of that later.

He or she may make impulsive decisions. Sudden engagements and proposals of marriage before the best time might sound romantic, but can end up causing you to act too quickly. Conversely, a quieter type might procrastinate horribly, mulling over all the pros and cons (YOUR pros and cons, maybe!) and agonizing about what the right decision would be. Does it mean you aren't loved enough? Not at all. Yet it is likely to become frustrating for you.

Two areas that can be problematic for anyone in a relationship with an ADHD-sufferer are money issues such as debt, and unplanned pregnancies. All of this has to do with impulsivity and trouble when making decisions.

Money is a fighting point in many relationships. On top of this, you have to add an extreme reluctance to do mental arithmetic in some people with ADHD, because they can't remember amounts or visualize abstract concepts well. Take a moment to stand in his or her shoes: can you imagine oranges or apples? I would be surprised if you couldn't. Now try to picture seven oranges. Then try to picture seven apples... you have to make sure you are seeing seven. I do it by seeing three pairs and an odd one. Yet what are you imagining? "Seven." It's an abstract concept. It's not the same as physical fruits, but it can exist in them. For you, this will probably be possible; if your brain suffers from ADHD, it's much more difficult. Many teachers of abstract subjects don't seem to know how to explain them. Do you really just put it up on the board or the screen and assume it's self-explanatory? Would they ever try to teach you as a child to see numbers in pairs in your mind, with an odd one where necessary? It's certainly implied in early-learning materials, but I believe victims of ADHD (and sometimes I do call them "victims", though that's no criticism) and anyone who struggles with abstracts, needs to learn those skills consciously later on in primary and middle school.

When emotional control is difficult and arithmetic is confusing, shopping and budgeting tend to give in to impulse buying. Once more, I plead with those of you who don't suffer from ADHD to understand that although someone can give in to an unreasonable impulse and make an extravagant purchase out of carelessness or pure selfishness, those aren't the only reasons for this behavior. Your partner with ADHD can be genuinely unaware of the consequences of spending money on something, caught up in the excitement of having found it. I don't mean to excuse unreasonable behavior, but I do want to help you understand it better. Shopping isn't simple – do you ever go around a shop with a calculator on your phone, working out how much products are per kilogram? Personal finance can be horribly complicated: loans, repayments, savings, income from one or several jobs, plus all the spending opportunities. Spare a thought for your partner. Must you take over, then? You must get involved, but no, taking over is not the best solution.

What human feeling is more impulsive and powerful than sex? We know this, but often fail to remember that it involves a lot of decisions. Am I ready for this? What will it feel like? And afterwards? Do I need to be more committed to go this far? Have I thought about having children? Do I know him or her well enough? And so on. People with ADHD have a very hard time making lists of pros and cons. Of course they generally know about the consequences of relationships and sex, but making decisions can be agonizing. Either they may avoid making them, until consequences come along, or else they fall head-over-heels in love and throw caution to the wind.

Research shows that ten percent of teenagers and younger women in a given society have had an unplanned pregnancy, compared to forty percent of ADHD-affected teenagers and younger women from similar backgrounds. Low self-esteem and having few friends must be among the reasons.

I don't want partners of people with ADHD to condemn their partners for what they might have done in a previous relationship, especially if they've had a child or children. I do want you to realize that love is about communication: talking about what you want, what you feel, what you think even when you aren't sure of it, and what you've done in the past. You wouldn't be reading about ADHD if you didn't care about the person who has it. You will need to be open and understanding.

It's also true that the impulsivity and the tendency to seek thrills mean that ADHD sufferers have been shown to have affairs more often than neurotypicals. Again, I don't mean to excuse bad behavior, but I do want to show why ADHD victims are prone to it, as they are to addictions.

Some of this has to do with what an impulse is. Seen against a confused babble of memories and facts that surrounds every ADHD sufferer, and against the backdrop of all the organizing that is so hard to do in the mind, an impulse is crystal clear. It's so simple, and can look just like a clear, attractive idea. How tempting, how beguiling!

The impulsive behavior seen with money tends more towards gambling with men, with figures possibly being easier for them – and consequences harder to see than they are for any neurotypical. What ADHD sufferers buy on impulse does seem to vary depending on being male or female, but I don't see that as significant in itself. Society might seem kinder to female impulse buyers when it doesn't think of them as providers, but many neurotypical women don't understand the depth of confusion that led to Emma buying an Italian handbag. They might say, "I know. Oh, just don't take me to Milan! I'd go crazy." However, on hearing that she couldn't pay for her daughter to get dental treatment, as a result of her impulse, the attitude changes to condemnation. "Selfish bitch! Splashing out on herself and making her child go without!" If Emma had bought a sports car, she would probably be treated much more harshly than a man who had made the same purchase.

A man who fathered a child as a teen generally has an easier time escaping shaming and condemnation than the mother. Part of this stems from the fact that the mother will almost always end up with the baby. When older, and beginning a new relationship, he might choose to hide the fact that he had a child as a teen. A woman who had a child and gave him or her for adoption could hide the fact, but having faced the guilt of all this, is more likely to want to share the truth, to apologize, you could say.

I don't want partners of people with ADHD to assume their partner is going to be unfaithful. I do want you to know some of what goes through the minds – or doesn't – of those who are affected.

What other developments can take place over time in a romantic relationship that ADHD can endanger?

You may end up losing your partner's "hyper-focus." It's possible that all of you, so to say, is too much for your partner to concentrate on. Or, the hyper-focus may go back to being your ADHD partner's pet subjects. Where once he arrived only slightly late and spoke of all sorts of things from food, to travel, to politics, to his family, some months down the road he may arrive terribly late and spend the whole evening talking his vacations. You will begin to feel your date has turned into a travel agency visit.

Further down the road, perhaps after marriage and a child or children, things will change if you and your partner don't work together to understand each other. Problems with depression can be made worse when you start to put a lot of time and effort into a new baby, for example. If your ADHD partner struggles to order daily life, you will start to wonder if the new business venture he spoke of will ever become reality. Will she ever get the job she talks so much about? If he's always helping other people and is never at home, you might think he no longer cares about you. After five years of his forgetting your birthday, will you feel unloved and forgotten?

We don't want to deceive a new date, but all of us are on our best behavior then. At some time that has to give way to the reality of who we really are. This is when tiredness and misunderstanding can trigger outbursts in a victim of ADHD who would have been much more patient with a new romance.

What can begin as two people helping one another (after all, aren't men and women made slightly different so they can complement each another?) can develop into what some psychologists call a "parent-child dynamic." The non-ADHD partner can be nurturing of the other, but not really treat him or her as an adult. The partner with ADHD can either surrender mentally and act childishly, or resent not being treated as an adult. Either way, this dynamic is not healthy.

I don't want to give you the idea that dating, staying together with, or marrying a person with ADHD is dooming you both to unhappiness. A good relationship is possible. But there needs to be openness and communication from the beginning. Often, an ADHD sufferer will be half-aware of his or her problem and try to hide it. It's caused deep shame and provoked unending criticism, after all. However, such an avoidance is not healthy. It's a refusal to communicate. Part of learning new strategies with

ADHD is attaining healthy self-esteem and avoiding negativity. This is the subject of the next chapter.

A Questionnaire - Does He or She Have ADHD?

As we know, you must consult a professional to know the different types of, and experience the severity of actual ADHD. There are also other neurological problems that can be suffered together with ADHD, or your partner may have one of these instead. However, these questions will help both of you. Some are for you, others for your spouse or partner. People of good will who knew him or her in childhood might also provide some informative responses.

Write down your answers, and take time afterwards to come back to them. Some of these questions may deal with things your partner may not have a problem with at all – individuals with ADHD are very variable. However, you should begin to see a clear pattern if your partner really does have ADHD.

FOR YOU

1) Is your spouse or partner currently having difficulty in personal interaction with someone (you or anyone else) that makes them very emotional; or in doing paid work (organizing, finishing, accuracy); or at home where work needs to be done and things maintained?

2) Is he or she habitually late for arrangements? Often in a last-minute rush? Does she/he show acute embarrassment at being disorganized? Is there a habit of totally underestimating the time needed to do something, as though if once imagined, it's done? The mind just races ahead of the body and the world...

3) Does your partner have a tendency to start projects, jobs, sudden inspirations, but fails to finish them? Do they have good ideas, but are very impractical about putting them into practice? DO they not bother to read instructions? Do you see that he or she becomes bored very quickly?

4) What's he or she like in conversation? Perhaps very talkative, but rushed, often changing subject mid-sentence? Does your partner interrupt you with a frantic desire to say something before it's forgotten? Or perhaps their stories are very long-winded and detailed, almost "school-teacher-ish?" Or are they silent and distant-looking, seeming to drift away and lose track of what you are saying? Can he or she be sometimes lively, entertaining and energetic, at other times dull, inactive and moody?

5) Does he or she either have to plan everything beforehand so as to achieve it; or are they someone who does best when improvising? Does pressure get the best out of them?

6) When your partner loses his or her temper, is it out of proportion to the crisis? Is it sometimes a rant that's still going on an hour later, or a sudden earthquake of rage that's often out of

proportion to the severity of the problem? Does he or she become full of tears and angry insults... then feel bad afterwards?

6) Does your partner ever become so engrossed or paralyzed by a task, they can't pull their attention away from it? Do they become angry and upset, or get a fright if they're interrupted? Some sufferers forget to eat; others have been known to damage their bladders because they won't break off what they're doing to go to the toilet. Is your partner ever like this?

7) Was your partner either restless and overactive as a boy or girl? Maybe he could never sit still; perhaps she always looked out of the window. Small distractions are not small for people with ADHD. If his or her classmate coughed, it took their attention off the teacher. If a crow squawked outside in the tree, they had to look outside. Can people who knew your partner say that he or she was like this before the age of twelve?

8) Have you ever experienced your partner being tactless or asking inappropriate questions about others' lives? Or does he or she seem to have an individualism that forgets to consider other people, but doesn't seem like deliberate carelessness?

9) Could you describe him or her as "often depressed?" Is he or she getting any treatment, or did they in the past, for depression? Has your partner ever said that he or she felt suicidal, now or at any time in life?

10) Does your partner struggle to remember facts, arrangements and names, etc.? Can you see that it bothers them to be forgetful? Has he or she been like this all through their life? At the same time, does he or she seem to have a strangely good recall of the past, or when dealing with a pet subject or interest?

11) Does your partner have any unusual reaction to drugs or foods? For example, coffee makes him sleepy/turns him into an overexcited "teenager"; one glass of alcohol and she's bubbly, restless and laughing a bit over the top, or crying? Is he or she hooked on any stimulating or depressant substance? Is he or she a "chain-smoker?"

12) Have you been worried by your partner doing any physical activity that looks dangerous, thrill-seeking, or extreme? This could be sports, mountain-climbing, travel in remote areas, etc. Has he or she suffered an accident or been in serious trouble to the point that you wonder if they are doing it properly?

13) Has he or she ever had accidents while driving or using machinery? Did it seem to be caused by a failure to concentrate? Does your partner suffer from any co-ordination problem? Or does he or she seem to have no sense of danger?

14) Does he or she hate loud noises or specific sounds, e.g. screeching metal, seagulls? What about disliking strong smells or tastes, or the feeling of certain fabrics? Does your partner sometimes blurt out his or her disgust, e.g. "Ugh! That's horri-

ble!", "That smells like ****," and so on, which can be embarrassing for you in company? On the other hand, are they absolutely crazy about some fragrance or substance, e.g. mint, or some taste or flavor, or some type of music that they listen to quite loudly?

15) Has your partner got into habits like compulsive porn use? Is your partner hooked on gambling? If so, is he able to tell you calmly how much he bets, and on what, without it seeming that he's getting irritated, hiding something, and that you're interrogating?

16) What are his or her sleeping patterns like? Is he or she someone who sleeps only a few hours per night, and seems tired during the day, but still doesn't sleep well? Is he or she a restless sleeper who wakes many times in a night? Or, does your partner sometimes sleep more than 10 hours even though they haven't done any unusual work or gone without rest for an unusually long time? Is he or she sometimes almost impossible to wake up?

17) Does your partner battle to start a job or project, becoming paralyzed by having to make a decision? Does he or she become agitated, or absolutely frozen with fear when looking at all the possibilities? E.g. "I don't know if I should take A or B – I can't make up my mind!" When he or she does work on something, do they either make lots of little errors, or else fuss about every detail to the point of slowing it down?

18) Do they struggle to tell the difference between an important part of a task and an unimportant one? In other words, your partner may spend a lot of time in a test answering one question in detail, then has five minutes left to do ten questions. Or maybe shredding mountains of spinach while letting the saucepan of water to boil it in go dry?

19) Does your partner either procrastinate badly, or get a sudden rush and wants to start immediately, putting other things aside in haste?

20) With your partner, is it always about extremes? Either your partner is VERY some way, or NOT AT ALL. ADHD is a disorder of balance. Some sufferers lean one way, some the other, and yet others again, swing. However, all of them have a brain that experiences a serious problem with organizing and deciding.

If your partner seems to be described in at least five of these question areas, then it's likely that he or she has ADHD or a related condition. This isn't an official test – please get some professional help, and by all means carry on reading this book, and finding other useful information.

FOR YOUR SPOUSE OR PARTNER

If you don't have ADHD, then you are all right! And if a professional looked at your answers to these questions, and your partner's answers to his or her questions, and says that you do, you're still all right! ADHD isn't anyone's fault, and there is a lot that people who have it can do about it. Knowing what your problem is might seem like having a good brain-wave, something that makes sense at last. Don't feel bad about yourself – people with ADHD can be successful and intelligent, and can actually do some things better than average. There are many ways for you take charge and manage your life better.

As you proceed through this questionnaire, you could just listen and answer as your partner reads you each question; or you could read them yourself; or you could read, and then write down your answers. It's up to you.

1) Can you say without having to think too much: I struggle with everyday life?

2) Do you have trouble slowing down or shutting off your mind, when you've been thinking about something? Does your brain seem to race ahead, and you can't stop it? Does something that makes you angry cause you some vivid and strong imagery that runs quickly and grabs all your attention?

3) Were you restless or overactive as a boy or girl? Maybe you could never sit still; perhaps you always looked out of the window. Small distractions are not small for people with ADHD. If your classmate coughed, it took your attention off the teacher. If a crow squawked outside in the tree, you just had to look

outside. Can people who knew you then, say that you were like this before the age of twelve?

4) Do you get new ideas, or realize things all at once? Examples: do you have a habit of remembering where you left your keys at odd moments, say, in the middle of making a sandwich? Do you remember what someone's name is while busy reading about bee hives?

5) "Write down your suggestions," they say. When you do, you get more and more ideas while you try to write the first one down, so you try to get those onto paper or the computer as well, and it turns into a complete clutter of ideas, with descriptions not finished, or muddled up?

6) Does it seem as if the people you are closest to are always complaining that you don't give them enough attention? Do they make you feel exhausted by their demands?

7) Do you often feel depressed? Feel that you have no energy or desire to get up and deal with a new day? Have you ever had ideas of committing suicide? Have you ever tried to get, or had, treatment for depression?

8) Would you describe yourself as someone who likes to be his or her own boss? Are you self-employed, or at least working where you don't have to be put in a straitjacket of other people's rules, times and expectations?

9) Have you always felt "different?" Did other kids think you were a bit odd, or a bit "spaced-out," or did people keep telling you that you made "too much of a fuss" about stuff they took calmly?

10) Be honest with yourself. Don't think about how you are going to explain it to your partner until later. Ask yourself: have I got into habits that I can't control? Like compulsive porn use or gambling? If your partner asked you about habits such as these, would it seem that he or she was interrogating you? Could you stop these activities for two months, and feel OK?

11) What about eating certain foods? Are there things you just can't resist? Does that make you feel really stupid and greedy afterwards?

12) Did you feel useless, confused, and depressed when younger because of the way adults – parents, teachers, etc. – kept on correcting you and telling you to "try harder," "put more effort into" something, and to "concentrate!?" Do people still talk to you with these words?

13) When you like doing something, like watching videos or going to parties, is it so good that you literally can't tear yourself away? Is it like an escape from all the bother and the mess of your own life?

14) Do you get bright ideas to help other people when you see what their situations are like – a solution seems obvious to you, and you want to help, but they become irritated with you? Do they challenge you about the stuff you're battling to put right in your life, and that hurts?

15) Are you someone who hates making decisions? You literally become paralyzed by worrying about them. Or do you get an idea in your head, and it's so good, so clear, you just want to start right away? Do people become critical when you have these inspirations?

16) Do you ever find some noise or taste or smell so irritating or disgusting, that you've blurted it out, "Yuck!", "I hate x...", "How can anyone put up with y...?" ...before you've even thought about other people's reactions?

17) Can you sleep more or less the same hours every night? Do you have frequent problems with going to sleep, or with waking up, or do you often wake in the middle of the night?

18) Do you often start doing one thing and forget about it? Such as the food in the oven while you vacuum the carpets, or the car running in the driveway because you saw your two children having a fight, and got out to deal with it...?

19) Do you ever want to shout and scream because people keep on criticizing you when you try to explain yourself and

describe the kind of problems you're being asked about in this questionnaire? "But doesn't everyone... forget something... lose their temper suddenly... drift off or fall asleep when it's deadly boring... get sudden inspiration... put something off because it's disagreeable?" For you, this is so much worse!

20) Can you say that you struggle with at least five of the areas mentioned here?

If so, it's likely that you have ADHD, or one of its related conditions. Once again, this isn't an official test – please get a professional opinion. Why not read this book, and look for other useful information together with your partner?

PART 2 - ADHD EFFECT ON RELATIONSHIPS

CHAPTER 4: MAINTAINING CONFIDENCE IN A RELATIONSHIP WHEN YOUR SIGNIFICANT OTHER HAS ADHD

When you consider the effects of ADHD as a child, and the ways in which other people consistently misunderstand and misinterpret the behaviour that it causes – especially when it isn't the "classic" boyish hyperactivity – you will guess correctly that it undermines self-esteem in sufferers and damages their confidence in social interactions.

In the 1950s and '60s, Eric Berne developed his theories of personality. His themes are psychological states and styles of personal interaction, and the method is known as Transactional Analysis.

Berne discerned four basic life positions, which are characteristic attitudes to the self and to others. In my view they are totally relevant to the problem of self-esteem I've just outlined. How you operate from each position will affect the way you handle other people and organize your own mind. These are the four positions:

- *I'm OK and you're OK.* This is the best position and the most mature way to approach life. It means that I accept and value myself, and that I also feel good about others and their talents and achievements.

- *I'm OK and you're not OK.* People in this position feel good about themselves but see others as inferior, worthless, as objects. It's a really narcissistic, "Cluster B" attitude, and this is not healthy for others or for them.

- *I'm not OK and you're OK.* A person with this life position sees him- or herself as the weaker partner when in a relationship. It's a depressed or neurotic state of mind where the person fears, or even believes that others are all better than themselves. Someone in this position may not resist abuse and might just resign himself or herself to it, saying that better is either not possible, or even that it's not deserved.

- *I'm not OK and you're not OK.* This is a sort of nervous breakdown, or a psychotic or paranoid state of mind. It's the worst position to be in, because it implies that the victim feels bad and useless, but also doesn't believe that there's any hope from the rest of the world.

When you look back at the experiences of people who live with ADHD, you can see that it's likely for them to grow up with the "I'm not OK and you're OK" type of psychological standpoint. Berne's techniques involve identifying your inner position and the ways it makes you behave maladaptively, sabotaging yourself or being mistreated by other people. Your goal is to see and interact with the good in yourself and in others. This doesn't imply turning a blind eye to your or anyone else's shortcomings; it's about being able to see reality and so to solve them.

Why is this so important? It's because anyone who has poor self-esteem will run into problems in romantic relationships. If you don't know how to receive love or feel unworthy of it, how will you give it? Would you know what it is you are going to give? This could apply to the respect and care that all familial and social relationships need to thrive, but here the focus is on romantic relationships. It has been demonstrated that beginning a relationship with poor self-esteem results in significantly less satisfaction with that relationship as time goes by.

The commandment, "love your neighbour as yourself" is highly relevant. Don't we emphasize the first part sometimes, and forget the second? It follows that if you don't love yourself, then you can't love others properly, maturely or happily. Maybe we trip up because we think that having self-esteem (loving yourself, properly understood) is to be like the "I'm OK and you're not OK" psychological standpoint. Such an attitude isn't self-esteem at all. It isn't love, period. Thinking of people as enemies to be destroyed or puppets to use, turns an abusive or manipulative person into an angry, vengeful, and bitter man or woman. Such people will ruin their partners' lives, and also their own happiness before long.

Self-esteem suffers when childhood is traumatic and family life is bad. It also suffers when there are personal problems, poor health and other difficulties in our early years. Am I implying that ADHD is caused by growing up in a dysfunctional family? Not at all! I want to make it clear again, as I outlined in the second chapter, that ADHD is an inherited, genetic disorder that does not result from bad mental experiences. Although some psychiatrists diagnose it with a different origin – after an accident or injury, for example – again, this is physical damage to the brain and not because of someone's poor decision, or a lack of love.

However, can children with ADHD grow up damaged and traumatized when their family is unsupportive, disorganized and unloving? Of course – it makes life worse for such a victim. Any deep childhood trauma causes many issues in later life, whether someone is neurotypical, has ADHD, or another disorder.

It is also possible for a basically loving, quite supportive and consistently disciplining family to give a boy or girl with ADHD a reasonable home, I believe, but not to understand what the problem is. Then, outside the home he or she suffers ridicule, struggles to achieve or to understand the surroundings, and is rejected by his or her peers. Perhaps other adults criticize and abuse these victims. The result? Trauma. Home might be a refuge, but these sufferers' sense of failure will not be cured. Such people, grown up, might have sustained less damage – but still have untreated ADHD, even severely.

Your spouse or partner might be one of these people. It seems to me that this is more likely than that he or she came from some kind of nightmarish, horror-story background. If that were the case, he or she might not understand love at all, or even ridicule and reject the idea of love, mocking the very ideals of a relationship. That you have got as far as you have is a sign that he or she can love – but loving when you're broken inside is often marred by failure and frustration for both parties.

The seeds of confidence or insecurity are sown in childhood. People who live with ADHD usually remember becoming aware at some point that they were "different" in a certain way, that there was some kind of "hole" or "flaw" inside them. Their reactions may not all be the same, but when one takes into account the difficulty they have in concentrating, co-operating generally, waiting or communicating, and all the criticism they get, it usually turns into a feeling of inferiority. Not only of being lesser than their peers, but also alone, separated somehow. Their different reactions and cognitive struggles will be different from those of their peers, after all. We have seen how it can be hard for them to see life from others' point of view, just as it is for others to understand theirs. They are different, and they're not hallucinating. ADHD does separate sufferers, it's a fact.

This is similar to the feelings of rejection the physically deformed or disabled may endure as children. However, in some ways it's worse, because the reason is not obvious. Do we expect people with Down's Syndrome to understand our emotional reactions? Usually not, to a fault. We actually assume they are not able to understand us, when many of them can and do. We judge based on who we see. In the case of a healthy, average or good-looking girl or boy, we assume that she or he has no problems, and are suspicious when they behave oddly in our eyes.

Perhaps ADHD sufferers see when they're worrying or bothering their parents and other members of their families. If they have siblings without ADHD, it is easy for them to spend their time comparing ("My sister always gets good marks"; "The boys laugh when she tells jokes..."), or hearing frustrated adults doing it ("Why can't you keep your eyes on the ball, like your brother?")

Two reactions can happen in their personalities; both are unhealthy for relationships. Some victims become defensive and angry, looking for and demanding some kind of comfort from other people. Others become depressed and angry, trying to avoid other people, yet longing for acceptance. Perhaps these would be the Hyperactive and Inattentive types respectively, but I think this is not always the case and you shouldn't assume it.

Defensive sufferers try to get confidence by seeking any kind of attention. That could include getting into trouble or picking fights. We have seen that drugs, sex and alcohol offer some kind of natural feeling of confidence. Alcohol in social settings give some people "Dutch courage" (apologies to the Dutch). Drugs taken in situations with other people can provide a sort of escape, a common ground on which to interact. Sex is one of the most powerful of natural "high" feelings. Might a girl who feels unloved and alone throw herself at the boys to get some kind of love and attention? Of course. Will a boy chase after girls to get the feeling of being better, braver and more desirable? Yes, he will.

I'm not justifying bad behavior, but I have to explain its extra lure and power but for people with ADHD. We know what the results are: disappointment. Drugs cause so many problems, as the "high" wears off, or turns into a "low." Alcohol provokes fighting, arguing, or leaves one with a hangover. Uncommitted, unloving, promiscuous sex causes VD, unplanned pregnancies, "low" feelings, fighting, arguing, and more: the "morning after" effect.

Despite these experiences, the body and brain remember the good feelings they sensed during their flights into escapism and pleasure, and when life looks grey and cold again, the desire to escape returns.

The effect of escapism on relationships is disastrous. You might be looking at this now. To help both of you, you must realize what the cycle of addiction is and accept, where relevant, that it's part of your partner's problems, and yours by extension. Addiction will be controlled not just by avoiding pleasurable, dangerous situations and substances, but by working on your partner's hidden wounds of low self-esteem. Do you realize that the cycle of defensive, pleasure-seeking activities leaves him or her with lower self-respect and a greater feeling of failure than before? In turn, that leaves your partner vulnerable to trying more and more extreme activities, trying harder drugs, crazier and filthier thrills, and drinking more and more, daring to risk health, finances and close relationships, because the pleasurable effects keep diminishing as the ADHD sufferer (or any other addict) gets used to the stuff…

You may feel like hitting him or her over the head – really, I do understand. But attempts to shame, belittle, control, or just scream and shout at a defensive, thrill-seeking ADHD partner are doomed to fail. Please, don't do it! In the next two chapters, I'm going to cover the ways to help and to manage ADHD together. Keep reading.

I am also concerned that the depressed and angry type of victim, trying to avoid other people, yet longing for acceptance, is over-looked here. These people first try to keep others at a distance. However, they can be clever, resourceful and sociable, and they have a deep need for human love and company. That's part of being human, after all. They also seek to escape. They, too, may turn to drugs, alcohol and promiscuous sex as an escape from low self-esteem. The way they take these or what they do may look different, but it will lead to exactly the same set of prob-lems, and end up undermining and damaging their self-image even further.

Suicide attempts are possible when self-esteem is damaged. A depressed victim of ADHD is obviously angry with himself or herself. Shouting, "You don't make sense!" or, "You're a failure!" or, "Why are you messing up our lives?" is only saying what he or she is already saying inwardly to him- or herself. Namely, "I don't make sense!", "I'm a failure!", and "Why am I messing up our relationship?"

In a relationship, someone with ADHD has to accept the diagnosis. The issues with self-esteem have to be admitted. Understandably, sufferers may be unwilling to do this. It conjures up images of crying buckets and dredging up the past, with all the things they are ashamed of both then and recently.

Maybe the issues in your relationship are not drugs, alcohol and unfaithfulness. Maybe he or she hasn't ever actually tried to commit suicide. However, this is not to say that you can ignore problems of low self-esteem. Nor is it to say that your ADHD partner can thrive if he or she avoids these issues on the basis that they "aren't that bad," or might endanger the relationship if you knew about them. They are more likely to affect your relationship negatively if they are not admitted, than if they are. Loving him or her shouldn't be conditional on keeping up appearances. If you are reading this because you have a partner or spouse with ADHD, I hope you will understand how it makes some kind of sense, and that the truth may hurt a little, but soon it will heal. Really, it doesn't hurt as much as running away from it does, and has, and could, and would. Let me encourage you to communicate that to your partner.

Because having low self-esteem makes ADHD victims very sensitive to criticism, you will need to play your part as lovingly as you can. You need to work at helping him or her to re-learn how to think of themselves. You are probably aware that more extroverted, defensive sufferers are just as sensitive as are shy, nervous and avoiding personalities. That having ADHD is not anyone's fault is so important that you must repeat it not only to your partner, but to yourself, over and over again. Saying so may not be a magic key to unlocking a solution for him or, but it will do its job. Together with understanding that the condition is treatable and manageable, that he or she has so many other talents and so much good personality, self-esteem issues can be grown out of.

Emotional issues are just as important for your relationship. Whether your partner seems distant and unaware of your emotions, or if he or she seems not to express his or her own, you both need to understand that this relates to self-esteem. Quieter, inattentive sufferers may feel a burning lack of confidence with expressing their own emotions. After tension increases over time, they may burst out in anger and fear, revealing their emotions suddenly. This can become a vicious cycle, shame resulting from their lack of control causing them to try to suppress their showing of their moods. They will face another hurdle trying to evaluate and handle your emotions, because it's difficult for them. Only practice can improve their empathy, but it can be easier to avoid thinking about your expressions and emotions entirely. The effect will be a lack of confidence, and low self-image.

Hyperactive or restless ADHD sufferers, or anyone who becomes outwardly defensive of self, can decide to ignore others' feelings. Boredom is something ADHD sufferers often experience, because concentration exhausts them. Why hide it, if that, too, is a strain? They will know that they could be hurting and angering you, but it would seem like the lesser of two evils. At least people will know what they are thinking, they'd say. However, the upset, conflict and misunderstanding only grow from such behavior. The result is the very same problem, arrived at by a different route: low self-esteem. They are not unaware of the misunderstandings. They, too, feel like failures, and are more sensitive that they dare to admit.

You see, the problems of anyone with ADHD are issues with poor self-control. How does that link to self-esteem? Victims of this disorder just don't trust themselves. It is so easy to be generally pessimistic and doubt one's ability in such circumstances. When conflict arises because of lateness or not doing household chores, to give two examples, a spouse or partner may lash out when criticized. It's defensive, more than an attack on you. Deep down, they feel unreliable. Being kinder and helping them seems to be the answer, but as I am going to explain further in the following chapter, it's nothing more than a temporary fix, because it just seems to re-enforce and confirm to the ADHD partner that he or she is useless and inferior.

A general vicious cycle can be seen in many behavior problems we humans suffer from. We struggle to cope with a situation, feel bad about our poor performance, and start either to avoid it or we deal with it badly. From this we set ourselves up for future failure, coming to expect it as normal, and then confirming it the next time we have to confront that challenge.

Self-esteem is at the heart of the problem, and is the way to advance out of it.

CHAPTER 5: NAVIGATING A RELATIONSHIP WITH A PARTNER WHO HAS ADHD

There are many ways to manage your relationship with someone who has ADHD. I will mention the basic fault, and thereafter some other common problems. Once I've identified each one, I will go on to show you some solutions.

The "Parent-and-Child" Communication Style

This is the single, biggest, most aggravating and intimacy-killing dynamic when one partner has ADHD and the other doesn't. To illustrate:

Little Frankie is three years old. When he wants to draw with crayons, his mom spreads a plastic sheet on a table and puts paper there together with his colored crayons. He loves drawing, using every page for his creations. He risks getting crayon on his clothes, so his mother puts an overall on him. When he's finished, she puts his pictures up in the kitchen for his dad to see when he comes home. The table is left in a messy state: crayons everywhere, some paper he tore up when a picture wasn't what he wanted; his overall is covered in colored stripes.

His mom takes it off him to put in the washing, and tidies the crayons, sorting out type A from type B and putting them in the right boxes. She throws away the waste paper, and rolls up the plastic sheet. There is a crayon-mark on the table leg that doesn't come off. When Dad comes home and proud Frankie shows off his artistic creations, Dad says to Mom, "Don't worry, I've got something to get that off," and cleans it away. Everybody's happy.

Next: it's Silvie's birthday party, scheduled for four p.m. on Saturday. At three p.m. her mother Janine is still trying to get all the preparations done. She loves having parties and loves Silvie to bits, but organizing is something she hates and it never seems to go right. Silvie's father Juan comes back from buying something, to find Janine in a complete panic: the birthday cake's still in the oven (Juan knows you have to ice them when the cake is cool...), and Janine suddenly says, "Oh, no! I forgot to tell Bella the party's starting at four. She thinks it's at five. I don't have any credit left on my phone!" Janine's starting to cry. So Juan says, "Don't worry, darling. I'm gonna help you."

He says he will buy a cake, and gets his wife's telephone. Quickly finding Bella's number and writing it down, he takes up the car keys from where he's just put them. As he starts up the car, he's calling Bella to tell her about the change of time. Twenty minutes later, he returns triumphantly from the bakery with a cardboard box that has an iced cake inside. Frantic Janine is so relieved. Her husband says, "Just make some extra icing for this. Put her name on it and some flowers or something. I'll look after the soda and the plastic cups."

This kind of thing happens often: Juan is used to it. Janine always says she doesn't need any help, and then she does, in the end. Bella thanks Juan for his call and screams silently. Soon she's frantically busy getting her son all ready to go. Janine is such a scatterbrain, she thinks. She, too, offered to help, but Janine always refuses.

Soon there are little kids running around screaming with joy. Juan is relieved now, also (he admits to himself alone) because he knows the cake won't be burnt, or taste of baking powder, as has happened at some other parties. Everybody's happy – or are they?

The third scenario: Chris is a total disaster at remembering things and organizing himself. He has a room in his flat that he has a desk in, for his computer and other paperwork, since he is a self-employed carpenter. His girlfriend has known him for six months, and she knows what happens when he forgets to go to see clients, charges the wrong amount, or has to rush to complete a big job because he didn't think of the time he would need for it. So, one day when she's stayed behind at his flat while he went out to work, she decides to tidy the desk for him. She sorts the papers into a pile, throws away the obvious rubbish (orange peel and plastic wrapping are surely trash), and removes the drill-bits, screws and the plane that have made their way onto the desk. These should be in the cupboard where he keeps his tools. (That's a disaster for another day, she says to herself). She takes away a large block of wood that's also ended up there, and puts it alongside the wall where he can see it but not have papers underneath it and over it. When he comes back, he's thankful, but rather casual.

"Thanks, Savannah. Did you find a diary on my desk? I've been looking, and I don't have it in my jacket pocket; I didn't see it anywhere."

"No, I didn't," she says.

"Where's that packaging? You didn't throw it away, did you?"

"That plastic packet?" asks Savannah. "I did."

"No! I need to get some more of those. They don't know what you want till you show 'em the packaging."

In the end he finds it in the trash. He can actually find some other things better now that his desk is neater, and she plans to ask him if she can look at his computer in the future. She would love to sort out the electronic clutter in there. She could be his secretary. Then everyone will be happy – or will they?

All three of these are situations where one person takes on the role of a parent, and sorts out life for the other one. Cryingly obviously, in the second and third scenarios, Janine and Chris are not children, but adults.

It's very easy for you, the non-ADHD partner, to try to help by playing the role of a parent to your ADHD-affected spouse, boyfriend or girlfriend. The big problem is that it's not going to be a relationship of two equals any more. Not only might he or she become overly dependent on you, but your partner may resent the way you control everything. You may end up shouldering an exhausting burden and find that you've bitten off more than you can chew. Frankie's crayons are far simpler than Janine's catering, her social networking and friends' circle, her marriage and her motherhood, taken all together. Chris might need a secretary, but how is Savannah going to help him without knowing every little bit of his disordered organizing? She must also ask herself: is she his secretary, or his girlfriend?

Once again, Eric Berne's theories of Transactional Analysis are relevant. His concept of "ego-states" explains how adults should be able to relate to one another as adults, but often our communications are not authentically adult-like.

Berne distinguished three inner "ego-states": "Parent", "Adult" and "Child." The "Parent" state is when we unconsciously mimic our parents, their actions and beliefs. The "Child" is a state in which we behave, feel, and think in a similar way to when we were in our childhood. The "Adult" state is when we look at reality and evaluate our emotions accordingly.

We can get into habits of thinking as a "Child" or a "Parent" as we grow up. This is not the same thing as being a young child, or talking to and interacting with a real, young child. It's a sort of false identity: if we live habitually in "Parent" mode it makes us begin to treat other adult people inauthentically by speaking to them as if they were children. Or we may think and respond to a romantic partner as if we were children without responsibility, if we live in "Child" state. It's common for ADHD sufferers to find themselves doing this. Examples of a non-ADHD partner being an "Adult" might be the kind of question one spouse asks another: "You do know it's Tuesday, don't you?" A "Child" might take a look at the total mess he's made in the house, and say: "Come on, honey. Let's go out for a meal. I can finish that later." An alternative strategy of an unhappy "Child" is when someone tries to disguise adult skepticism and irony by speaking as if he or she were an innocent child: "I know what: let's spend all our money on an expensive vacation. We can starve afterwards."

Being an "ego-Adult" is not always to be unkind or critical. Berne distinguishes carefully between sub-types of the states. There is a "Nurturing Parent" of which Juan and Savannah look to be good examples. Alternatively, there is a "Critical Parent" state. Be that as it may, as time goes on in a relationship and there are obstacles, challenges and stress, it often happens that a nurturing "Parent" becomes a critical one.

Many types and patterns of these communications have been demonstrated by Berne. I believe this Transactional Analysis is a useful tool to identify unhealthy dynamics in any relationship. It also applies to groups. In the end, the adult who is treated as a child is going to feel resentful, dependent and not respected. Conversely, the one who treats the other as a child is going to feel stressed, unfulfilled, unappreciated and frustrated. You must also recognise that there is no one single way of organizing most complex human activities. You might start changing things to your way, but if your partner could do exactly what he or she wanted, it might be very different. Adults need to talk to adults as adults, in adult ways. That's the underlying message and method of Transactional Analysis.

I don't mean to criticize everyone who finds themselves in Savannah's or Juan's situation. If you love someone and there is a sudden crisis, then you will do whatever you can, quickly, to help them.

That sort of "parenting" approach is a "quick fix", but it isn't a long-term solution. You need to find strategies to help you to assist – but not take over – and your ADHD partner needs to find strategies to learn the skills for life that an adult needs. Then the two of you must put them together so the strategies harmonize.

Attitudes: Don't Jump to Conclusions

Many problems for people with ADHD begin and continue because we are so quick to discern attitudes in them. If they don't do something well and they subsequently avoid it, we may think they are being "lazy." If they can't concentrate for long without huge effort, and drift off into silence for a rest, people say he or she's "aloof" or "cold." If they complain that something is hard when it is for us also, but we have no idea of how much worse their predicament is, some of us don't hesitate to say they're "spoilt."

As I cover five basic challenges a couple must face when one partner has ADHD, this question of attitudes touches on all of them. Try not to judge attitudes that may not be there at all – if your partner's symptoms are irritating, his or her behavior dangerous or irrational, focus on the behavior itself (what he or she did or didn't do) and not what attitudes it seems to convey. Make it clear why what she did caused you problems; tell him what actually happens because of what he says and does.

I will outline each basic problem and then share some guidelines and advice for dealing with it, and lastly some ideas for communicating more effectively. Some of this advice is for you, the non-ADHD partner; other guidelines are for him or her to put into practice.

Five Challenges for Both of You, and Some Strategies to Handle ADHD Better

1) INATTENTION AND CONCENTRATION DIFFICULTIES

One of the areas most deeply affected by ADHD is conversation, as is giving instructions. People living with ADHD keep losing their focus during conversations, often leading you, their partner, feel ignored or frustrated. Inattention has an unforeseen effect: it can also lead him or her to agree to do things without realizing what was agreed to! Or, things that are later forgotten much more easily.

Your partner needs skills to manage their attention, both as an aid when distraction makes holding attention harder, and also to help when he or she battles to take their attention off something they are hyper-focusing on in a given moment.

For example, your partner mustn't be shy to ask you to repeat yourself when he or she loses focus on what you're saying. They mustn't think they have to pretend that they hear everything. When listening to you, a good idea is for them to put down anything they were doing beforehand. Concentrate only on you, not the accounts, or the broken chair, or the cooking. On your side, learn to recognize when your partner's attention is lost. If you see this, stop briefly and wait, or check by asking a simple question, or repeat the important thing you just said.

ADHD sufferers have a tendency to stop working on one task suddenly and start another, without finishing the earlier one. Using calendars and even stopwatches and alarms can help here. When he or she is in the period showing on the calendar, or the time-frame of the alarm, they know they must be doing the present job, and not any other chore that might come into their thoughts. This can lessen the stress of feeling that many other things need to be done. Once the alarm rings, or it's a new day, they can start to wonder again about the other areas they need to give attention to.

Using drawings and images can help someone who is visually oriented to keep his or her focus. If they see a picture of a tree on the notice-board during the day, for example, they can remember they have to water the garden that day...

Some counselors and therapists recommend that people use "anchor words." These are words or phrases to help them to remember something, words that have an association. Having such words written up to see often, or being memorized for moments of confusion, helps to keep them focused on what is important. Such as, "jingle bells" to remind someone that someone is coming to fix the door chimes. In a moment of swirling thoughts about the Coronavirus statistics in Greenland, and more pressing, nagging worries, an ADHD sufferer might be able to recall and say those words: "Jingle bells, jingle bells... Why is that for today? Yes, it's because the handyman is coming to fix the door-chimes this afternoon."

Such "anchor words" or phrases can help someone who has lost track during a conversation, class or speech. They could write down some keywords in a lecture and to get their thoughts back to the topic at hand.

Relaxing is just as important for someone who suffers from ADHD. They find dividing the twenty-four hours of each day into work hours, sleep hours and family hours, to name some possible divisions, very hard. So when it's time to stop work or to enjoy a well-earned break, they need to disengage completely and stop thinking about all the things they haven't done, or must do the next day.

Here are some relaxation techniques to help your partner focus on relaxation – it will help them focus on organizing as well, when the time for that comes around again. Deep breathing exercises or meditation videos can make them feel calmer and simply not think about the stuff they've been doing for hours. Sometimes, prayer and meditation, good as they are, often feel like neurotypical guides for neurotypical people. However, good masters of contemplation and prayer, or mindfulness generally, are aware of focus and organizing. Maybe your partner will do better to walk in the park and practice meditation than sitting in a lotus position... perhaps the rosary or prayer beads are better used while walking down a busy street, than at home with candles lit; it could be that listening to CDs of Bible verses or Oriental wisdom is much better than trying to read them silently at your desk where you might just see that note telling you to put out the rubbish, and remember that you have to call your new client tomorrow... Other relaxation could be a time just to dream about the future, just drift off. This would be planned and scheduled, of course. This is only a problem when some ADHD victims do it at the wrong moments: other times it could be pleasant and inspiring.

Music helps many people. What kind depends on who your partner is; classical is so logical and ordered, you can do math to it; dance is wonderful for lifting your mood and helping you focus on cleaning the car, for example; heavy rock might fire you up to do better in the gym. Soft, hypnotic music helps many ADHD sufferers go to sleep – something many of them battle to do.

Sometimes actual chores such as washing the dishes or cutting the grass, help someone to focus on one task at a time and feel refreshed afterwards. Your partner must do what works for him or her. In work-related tasks, all of us find one or other aspect easier or more stimulating. Your partner can relax a bit doing this task, then return refreshed to the more taxing work.

Physical exercise is very beneficial for people suffering from tension and emotional pain, or tiredness from trying to concentrate. It benefits young ADHD victims and mature ones alike. It could be individual training such as gym workouts, or sports played with other people. Gardening and building work also fall into this category...

Reading can relax many people, depending on what the topic is. For some it will be fiction, for others, non-fiction. Some people do much better with a paperback they can take anywhere, even the beach; others will listen with far less distraction if it's an audio recording.

Focusing your attention in a time of modern, attention-grabbing devices is a topic all of us need to think about. Ask yourself if you are bothered by the number of times a day you now have to look at an e-mail, check a text message, or watch a video. Having good focus implies controlling the use of the internet and cellphones. It's necessary for you and even more so for your partner to make times where your phone's on silent, or not with you. After all, we lived without these mobile telephones for years! Not looking at your e-mails and messages helps you to focus on the real, non-message world.

You will notice that I've been very free with my suggestions. ADHD is a complex disorder, and affects different people in different ways. We human beings are varied and complicated. Your partner must find out what works for him or her. This is one of the reasons why you can't play the role of "Parent": you can help him or her to think better, but you can't think for him or her. You may find some of the techniques that your ADHD partner warms to are really odd and unhelpful for you. If so, respect their individuality and be happy that they do things that way. Be encouraging. If you feel that something isn't helping, say so and offer suggestions to make things better. If your partner doesn't agree, don't argue, but accept it for the time being.

2) DISORGANISATION OF TIME, MONEY AND TASKS

In practice, this is likely the most important area where your partner will need help and encouragement. It's the field where either ADHD is managed, trauma healed and communication flourishes, or frustration grows and self-esteem and confidence wither.

You might feel as if you have to do half the work your spouse or partner is supposed to do. Maybe you really do. To stop over-burdening yourself, and help him or her to be more effective and happy, I'll share some observations and bits of advice.

Keeping a diary or journal helps some people with ADHD think about how they are doing generally, and to see their progress, or lack of it, from a distance. The goal is not just to be ordered, but to lessen the feeling of being out of control that so plagues them.

What's the most important thing, right now? That is the question for your partner; also for you, because you don't want to end up fighting over a small detail because you've ended up over-focusing like he or she sometimes does!

Adults with ADHD need to find ways to simplify daily life, so encourage your partner to find ways to simplify their days. They need to give life's most important matters the majority of their time, which they are generally bad at without having gentle reminders.

Punctuality Is a Point of Pain

One of the most important organizational outcomes everybody has to manage is the ability to finish things on time, or to arrive at a given hour. ADHD sufferers are generally, unsurprisingly, bad at these things.

Interestingly, the symptoms of ADHD were described several hundred years ago, but not clearly distinguished and understood until the twentieth century. Hundreds of years ago, people had only clocks on steeples, and possibly the rich had inaccurate mantelpiece clocks and watches. Country people had dawn, mid-day and dusk before night. The angles of the sun... Who had to rush to meet someone at exactly 12.35 p.m.? Who panicked because her watch was ten minutes slow?

Modern life, with its armies of complicated, accurate machines and large numbers of people living close together, needs more timekeeping and organizing. An ADHD sufferer two hundred years ago might have had an easier time with life. They didn't benefit from electronic reminders on their phones then, but were there so many things to remember?

Our modern obsession with punctuality (in varying degrees across cultures) is just that: modern. People have always required self-discipline and expected some kind of timing, but we've gone overboard.

An ADHD-affected individual has to adapt to modern life, I know. We can't "magic" him or her back to the past. One thing you can do is not let assumptions turn you into a critical "Parent." Why do we fly into a rage with someone who is late, accusing them of deliberately trying to insult us by not bothering enough to arrive on time? If we ourselves are late, is it ever because we do it to provoke someone else? Sometimes? Never? The case of someone who just cannot care enough whether he keeps you waiting or not should be a case with far more evidence of arrogance.

How does someone who struggles with keeping to time manage his or her deadlines? This advice has proved really important to many people who are always late: when you feel that you have limited time, when the space you planned to use for some given task is running low, focus on the main task. Don't try to do everything!! There is a tendency for some people, especially ADHD sufferers, to realize they have so many more things to do. Feeling the pressure to get all those unfinished chores done, they frantically try to use the ten minutes left before some deadline to clean the floor, send an e-mail to the doctor, and write a note to the children. Oh, and to polish the shoes they're wearing! This results in a panic. In the end, only some of the chores are finished. Subtly, they get the feeling that chores are always frantic, and that planning never really works out as it should. That's a vicious cycle that needs to be "un-learnt" bit by bit.

How to Organize Your Life Better

If someone with ADHD tries a suggestion here, or any other piece of advice they've heard, and it doesn't help, say, "Don't be discouraged!" People really do learn from their mistakes, and they must not feel ashamed. Then one just moves on to try another suggestion.

Distraction is the greatest problem for those with ADHD of any type. This can be distraction by a memory or passing thought, or from an external event. To help with distracting thoughts and sudden memories (which may be good, but just not THEN...) your partner can use what some life-coaches call a "thought dump."

What's that about? Imagine you are frying fish in the kitchen, and suddenly you remember that you promised your cousin you would find her a CD from your collection. You get the point: you might just go off and spend fifteen minutes looking – and the fish goes black, or the frying pan goes up in flames. So what can you do? The CD is important.

You make a whiteboard or put a jotter-booklet in a prominent place, where you can zoom off and write a quick reminder. As the thought bursts into your consciousness, write a note so you can deal with it at a better time, i.e. when you aren't in the middle of frying. Then get back to your job. It's the other half of a "brainstorming" note.

The problem is that ADHD sufferers brainstorm most of the time, and so need not just to condense their rambling thoughts about something, but to keep their thoughts on other topics separated. This is a way to do it.

It sounds counterintuitive, but take short breaks. Literally, when he or she has to concentrate, e.g. study, they can set periodic alarms. When that sounds, stop studying at once. Researchers have found that this helps one to stop over-focusing, and get back to the right perspective. After the break, concentration is better.

Working with someone else is a method many people use to organize life. This person doesn't have to be you, the partner (though it might be). It could be a friend or colleague your partner can trust, preferably who understands ADHD.

This person mustn't take over, but they can help him or her to keep focused, encourage them when work feels exhausting, and be good listeners. Having someone there can help remind your ADHD partner that other people have expectations and needs – in a good way. This is the person you can plan with, where you can agree on the steps you will need to take to achieve an important outcome.

How about this: be your partner's "clutter companion." This is someone who helps another to sort things out. It must be a person who has knowledge of what your partner does. So, at intervals of maybe of a couple of months, the "clutter companion" helps them to sort a desk, computer, workshop, garage, kitchen or some other part of a home into... let us say, four piles: "Keep this," "Give away," "Throw away" and "I can't decide." The last one is important: sometimes you just can't say, and you don't want to stop dead in your sorting work. Come back to those ones another time.

Talk to your partner about what is needed in a situation. Does he or she understand the task at hand – or are they avoiding thinking about it, and just starting anywhere without even knowing what it's all about?

Such impulsiveness and avoidance is understandable because the task at hand can seem threatening or confusing. The job might look vast and exhausting because they aren't breaking it down into steps, and their motivation goes to zero. So, ask your partner some questions to help you both to gauge what needs to be done, and how.

Doing work in steps helps because it also provides mini-goals for your partner to celebrate, and to put the progress into perspective.

I know that people with ADHD hate deadlines. Most people who suffer from neurological deficits and problems do. But having no deadlines can actually make you waste time, and not focus your efforts. Distraction is harder to resist when you can tell yourself you still have time.

Help your partner to suggest realistic deadlines. They have to seem slightly long, to stop him or her from over-promising, which often happens because of fear and low self-esteem. Being near deadlines but slightly behind is better than being nowhere near them!

Organizing tools: everyone needs them. Someone with ADHD will benefit from notes and labels and displays, and electronic aids for everyday life. A whiteboard (or blackboard, if you're old-fashioned like me) is a wonderful, simple way for your partner to put up reminders for himself or herself. It's also a great way for you two to communicate with each other, and all other members of the family.

Clocks and alarms, and all the applications available for smartphones and computers, help to keep people focused during the day. I will mention some of the best apps later in this section. Some people need several reminders to remember an appointment, for example. That's not a problem – they can be set to go off twice or three times at definite intervals.

Little notes are good, but larger, diary-style entries are also useful. By this, I mean writing longer comments where someone highlights the most important goals, the eventual outcomes and milestones that a certain job features. Your partner might even like to write about how they feel about the job and the goals they have set for it. Being aware of your own feelings is important when you have ADHD; as it is for us all.

Be patient with your partner who lives with ADHD, but do put it over gently that untidiness is confusing. Once they realize that although tidying is difficult, it's also practically useful, it can motivate them to do it. When you are in tidier, uncluttered surroundings, you actually have fewer distractions, and you can work and think more clearly. A tidy environment is somewhere that has fewer unfinished jobs visible in it, or irrelevant objects and reminders.

Make a special time to get rid of old notes and reminders. They can build up so much that they start breaking down your organizing efforts.

Other Tips for Your Partner

- Put electronic tabs on your house-keys and in a purse that will bleep when you activate the central unit they come with, so you can find what you've lost.

- Put notes in prominent places. Try on the inside of the toilet door, or inside the front door to see as you leave home. Use bright-colored notes that are easy to see when you pass the place they've been pinned up or stuck.

- Have physical things to fiddle with, such as spinners, squeeze-balls, and so on. They might distract other people when you're with them, but on your own, they will relax you and let off your excess physical energy better.

- If you use a number of things for a certain task, such as a watering can, plant food and clippers, keep them all together.

- Use upcoming visitors as a way to get yourself to order and clean your home.

- Put notes in the places where the things they refer to are; such as a cupboard where the coffee-jar is. On the emptying jar, stick a note saying "Buy coffee."

- Put papers and clutter you don't have time to sort into large plastic bags. Add a label that says, "Sort this out" for later.

- Don't change the oil, pump the tires and wash your car all in one day: do each thing one day at a time. If you have to break the planned times because of unexpected events, you still got some of it done without killing yourself trying to do "car" for a whole exhausting day.

Phone Applications That Help With Overcoming ADHD Problems

Smartphones are terribly distracting, as I said, but also potentially very useful. A huge number of applications have been designed to help people with organizing life.

There are apps that help you in the following spheres:

- Grocery shopping and budgeting. You can write lists and set your budget, and enter the price of what you put in your shopping trolley or basket.

- Remembering passwords and personal numbers

- - Traffic and driving navigating, so he or she doesn't get lost. Or they can find the best way to avoid traffic jams.

- Relaxation videos and audio

- E-mail and calendar apps help you to sort out incoming mail and get reminders for each day, or a set time, to deal with the relevant e-mail or message.

- Calendar apps can put your lists and appointments all into one place, so you don't lose them or find yourself unable to gain access to them when all you have is your phone.

-

A spare telephone isn't an app. Yet it could be a life-saver if you forget your precious organizer phone. You can still make calls, and using some apps, you can get messages from the lost phone sent to that one.

- • - You can get apps to record voice-notes or text notes for later use, whenever you want to compose them.

There are so many helpful apps. Encourage your partner to try some and stick to the ones that work for him or her. You can even share apps that communicate between your partner's phone and yours.

You are warmly encouraged to work with and suggest things to your partner. But don't force your suggestions on them. Their organizing must be adapted by them, for them.

3) IMPULSIVITY

When we speak about impulsivity, we mean acting on sudden urges and wishes, interrupting conversations, and sharing feelings instantly, without stopping to think of the likely effect on listeners' own feelings. It's one of the direct causes of conflict in a relationship with someone who has ADHD.

One of the best ways for him or her to handle this trait is to learn to wait before they say something, or make a decision – especially when the impulse is emotional and rapid. You, as their partner, can help by asking if something is really as urgent as it feels. You can also ask them how the person your partner wants to say something to is going to feel about what they wants to say.

If someone with ADHD feels very angry or afraid, they could practice deep breathing for a minute or two. Then they must ask themselves what they actually feel like doing – and if that would really help. Some people make a resolution every morning to think about and clarify what their emotions are before they let themselves do what their sudden flashes of feelings suggest.

Making plans helps people channel their emotions better. If you have thought beforehand about what you will do and how you will feel if it works out one way, and how you would feel if it works out the other way, then you will handle either outcome with more logic and less panic and disappointment.

Some sufferers of ADHD, who are prone to talk rapidly and thoughtlessly, picture an imaginary lock or mask over their mouth. To speak, they have to think of it being unlocked carefully!

Impulse buyers could take you, or a good friend, with them on shopping trips. They can decide that the questions one has to ask them will be whether they need what they want to buy, how it will be useful and where it will go, and so on. Other people take pictures of what they've seen. They go home and look at them later before they decide to go back to buy them.

When there is a disagreement, people with ADHD need to concentrate on the matter at hand. It can be tempting for them to try to act against or oppose the personality of people they have disagreed with, instead of following the facts.

Maybe the most important time for them to hold back mentally is when they feel a strong sense of like or dislike for some other person, without knowing quite why. I'm still a believer in intuition, but this isn't an excuse for prejudice. ADHD sufferers always need to think about why they feel the way they do. Is there a more obvious reason for the feeling? Is it rational? Why would this person be of ill will? Or, why would they be secretly in love with me? Is the dislike – or feeling of admiration – the result of a past bad or good experience that has nothing to do with the circumstances and the person in front of me? If they can see that it is, they can act to control their thoughts and not do or say something they might regret later.

In your case, being the one who doesn't have ADHD, the thing to remind yourself as if by a mantra is: don't take it personally. When your partner says things tactlessly, or crudely, or even critically, just don't take it personally. They know they're saying something that conveys their emotions, but they live feeling as if they are the only sensitive people on the planet, and that everyone else is thick skinned. They need to understand this isn't true; yet you just have to think about their experiences during childhood to understand why life might look that way for victims of ADHD.

4) FORGETFULNESS

ADHD sufferers forget because they can't pay enough attention, and so they miss things. This isn't really forgetfulness, rather, it's never having known them. In addition to this, they can and do forget what they've understood and remembered on earlier occasions. Society and its expectations can turn neurotypical people into judges who come to expect that ADHD sufferers are forgetful.

Here are some organizing tips and advice for your partner:

Have an electronic calendar on your computer and telephones, that you share with your partner. Put in your assignments for work or study, your jobs around the house, your social life, anything and everything important. This way, when you have to pick up the kids from school, you will get a reminder. When you have to clean the bathroom, when your friends are coming around for a few drinks, you will get a reminder. Don't let your spouse or partner who doesn't have ADHD do all the jobs for you. However, they can remind you. Set up repeat alarms, for say, five or ten-minute intervals, for times when you are hyper-focusing and need those extra jolts to get you back into the world around you.

Similarly, a real, non-virtual, paper calendar in a prominent place is not outdated at all. You can make it a resource for the whole family. If you have children, encourage them to share in it by putting up their chores and activities too. You can check their activities and they can check yours! Kids are busy learning how to remember facts and arrangements, and often they forget, because it's new to them. However, they often remember things when adults don't, so encourage them and praise them when they help you in this way.

The first things anyone thinks of when you mention aids for your memory are notes, lists and reminders. Notes are wonderful: don't disparage them! Bright-colored reminders and lists of to-do jobs or purchases do need to be worked at to help someone effectively. Some ADHD sufferers feel discouraged by past failure with memory, or get an impulsive urge to do something without sitting down to draw up a list. It's wrong, but understandable. They are sometimes afraid that the concentration required will turn into a hyper-focus that will drag on for hours – or else a wild goose chase through their mind that will end up at the Pyramids of Egypt, by way of the Great Wall of China – when all they wanted to do was go shopping for groceries and get some fertilizer for the green beans in the garden!

Your advice here is: resist that urge. Sit down and make the list, but promise yourself that you are going to finish it quickly. If you remember something else while you are at it, write a note about that affair, stick it up, and carry on with the list. Then make sure you leave for the shopping without too much delay.

Of course, we enjoy lots of electronic, modern notes to help with life – some people e-mail themselves with information relevant to what they are doing, while they are at the computer. They'll pick it up later when they log in to read their e-mail.

For really important, confidential, offline information such as passwords, financial details or the location of the family treasure trove, why not have a notebook for it? No – two. One for you to hide, the other for your partner who doesn't have ADHD to hide. You know the saying, "Don't put all your eggs in one basket." Both of you need to check that the necessary information is in both booklets. Both need to know where both notebooks are.

Other people use a notebook as a vademecum that goes with them to work, or stays at home in an important place. Anything and everything goes in there. Yes, it could look confusing to your partner, but it's your store, and you will know it. Get a new one every year so the details don't become excessive. Keep the old one, just in case...

Because you, the non-ADHD partner, know that relying on memory alone is a no-go for your partner (is it so for anyone these days?) prepare how and when you are going to talk to each other to plan things together. When you fail to talk under the right circumstances, it's a likely to lead to more forgetfulness.

So, you, as the neurotypical partner in the relationship, make sure of the following: If you want to tell your beloved something important, ensure he or she has a notebook, phone or computer to note it down. If that isn't possible right there and then, do it later, and make a note of it for both of you.

Do you have enough time to do the planning? Are you both suitably focused? You might have to wait until the children are in bed, or even get up earlier in the morning. I know some people with ADHD don't sleep well, and aren't normally early risers. Yet I just suggest this because our minds and memories are often much fresher and less distracted in the morning after rising and washing.

Some people put up pictures to remind them to focus on a job or a goal. A picture paints a thousand words.

Other people journal/keep a diary where they don't just plan ahead or remind themselves, they actually evaluate their strategies. Literally, they look back at a week or a month and say, "Hey, how was that? Am I remembering better? What did I forget? What did I succeed in carrying out, remembering, etc.?"

When you remind your partner of something, time it sensibly and make it pleasant and "un-nagging." Nagging makes memorizing worse, not better, when you dump reminders on someone with words such as, "You need to call your father, AND you forgot to tell me his carer isn't able to come next week so we're going to have to help him; AND don't you realize we haven't got a lightbulb to replace the one that blew in the storeroom, AND why didn't you put up that picture you said you would...?" You actually confuse and worry your spouse or partner, which makes them forget more easily.

5) EXPLOSIVE TEMPER, IMPULSIVITY AND LOSING CONTROL OF EMOTIONS

Explosive temper seems to be a combination of impulsivity and trouble with concentrating. It's also a result of years of criticism. People with ADHD often burst out with emotional reactions: sometimes it's not anger, just tactlessness or even enthusiasm. At other times, and particularly in the cases of certain individuals, it's a serious problem with anger management.

The best bit of advice for him or her is not to act on sudden impulses. To do so is to act without thinking. People have to stop... and wait... and start thinking. What am I feeling, exactly? Why do I want to do this/don't I want to do this?

These are some logical, calming considerations to use in a sudden moment when emotions seem to be spiraling out of control:

- Most things we fear and imagine don't happen, or happen differently to what we over-visualized.

- Most things we daydream about or become over-excited about don't happen, or happen very differently to what we imagined.

- Ask yourself exactly what you are afraid of. If your spouse is late coming back from a family visit and hasn't called you, is it because a) there's been a plane crash, b) he's having an affair, c) the airport is very busy at this time, or d) there's a traffic jam on the way home? If you don't know, you don't know. Is calling his phone a good idea if he's driving? Why not wait for a while before calling? Ask yourself if he's really likely to be having an affair, or remind yourself that air accidents are far less common than people may think.

- When you completely lose your temper with someone, often it's because of some other worry or fear in the background. So, what is that? If you can identify it, you can start separating it from yourself, or focus on what the deeper problem is.

Controlling and directing your anger is an important skill. Consider finding and reading a guide on anger management to get some basic and some detailed strategies.

In the meantime, here are some other guidelines:

- If you are going to explode, go off to another room, go out for a walk, drive off – simply separate yourself from the surroundings and the person you're furious with. Then return and talk later, once you've had a chance to think about why you feel this way, and what you want to say.

- Don't suppress and squash down your anger: that doesn't work for long. It won't be long before you just can't carry on, and you explode. You have to express it, but must do so wisely.

- If you speak accusingly and aggressively, you invite someone to be defensive, and just carry on doing whatever angered you in the first place.

- Tell someone you are angry with how it makes you feel and why it makes you feel that way. Don't place blame so easily; tell them what went wrong instead. E .g. instead of, "You went against my wishes and told my sister about my operation," but rather, "Someone told my sister about my operation, and now she's worried sick. I feel bad that she knows I was hiding it from her."

- Recognise precisely what triggers you to start bellowing and shouting. Is it a screeching wheel on one of the kids' toys, or is it when you have a migraine? Take steps to solve those problems before they trigger you.

Moods and Expressions of Emotion

There are some moods and expressions ADHD sufferers often show; others they don't display clearly to those around them. Also, you as a non-sufferer show moods and expressions that they don't understand well or fail to see. For this reason, get into a habit of talking to each other about how you feel and why. Don't assume that it shows on your face.

Sometimes your partner will have a blank, expressionless face. That could be because they are really concentrating on you. Their thoughts race and their minds calculate very fast, so nothing goes out to their face to express it. It's just something you do with ADHD. He or she can try to become aware of this when listening to you, and simply blink or turn their head briefly, then re-focus on your face. It helps them keep their focus shining on you, and showing.

Further to this, at other times, ADHD people blurt out their likes and dislikes. This can be very embarrassing for everyone involved. Imagine being with a slightly overweight acquaintance at a clothes shop, and she's trying some new blouse or skirt, and your ADHD-affected partner says, "No way, that'll never fit you!" Or, they might not say anything verbally, but they might roll their eyes or sigh before you can say, "Stop!"

Yes, they need to practice their manners. Your partner could try to make a resolution before an important event: "I'm going to think first and then talk; I don't want to open my mouth and put my foot in it!" One has to get into the habit of being polite – of realizing that other people also have sensitivities.

Impatience is a huge challenge for many people living with ADHD. One cause of it is information overload. When they start to shift and look agitated, or frown a lot, and if it's in a situation where many things compete for one's attention, you know this is the reason. They may also think very quickly and with vast variety; it's an advantage at times, but it tires them mentally.

What can your partner do, and what should you do? He or she can let you know when it's too much. Communication is the key. ADHD sufferers need to take time off to recuperate and process what they've experienced. You can, from your side, train yourself to recognize their expression of tiredness and impatience.

Wrestling with communication can be irritating or exhausting for those who have ADHD. Sometimes people don't understand them when they think they've been clear; sometimes they are the ones who fail to get the point. Rather than show irritation, someone can make a slight smile with the mouth closed, deliberately, and breathe in. Then they can ask for clarity, or can repeat themselves. The effort of smiling takes away some tension, and stops them from seeming aggressive to the person they're talking to.

Embarrassment and fear can be intense for some sufferers. Blushing, panting and shaking can be signs that their body is under stress because of their mental exhaustion.

Be aware of these signs of distress in your partner. What can he or she do to relieve these unpleasant effects? Do quick breathing exercises. At first they might seem artificial and rather weird, but with practice they can be almost invisible to bystanders. They can calm your mind, slow their heartbeat and get their breathing back to a normal rate. Then they really will be able to deal with the situation better.

STRATEGIES TO COMMUNICATE BETTER

Any problem in a relationship is helped by better communication, and ADHD doesn't have to be an exception. Here are a few considerations relevant to ADHD-sufferers:

Being aware that your partner is probably hyper-sensitive is one step in communicating better with him or her. Hyper-sensitivity is often the result of enduring so much criticism and correction, and of the ADHD sufferer's reduced ability to ignore irritating sounds, sights and even thoughts. Some have extra-sensitive hearing and smell. Criticizing anyone fosters defensiveness, when what you want instead is to encourage openness. Nonetheless, you don't want to hide things from your partner: it's a case of being tactful, but open.

Love, attraction and intimacy are not possible when two people spend their time nagging, criticizing and bothering each other. That's being the critical "Parent," when what you need to be is a lover, not a mother-in-law or father-in-law. Anything said in an attacking tone invites retaliation rather than change or patience in an ongoing effort.

So, to communicate better, be open and explain yourself. Explaining yourself may sound negative, but it isn't the same as apologizing for your actions. It's about sharing your point of view and your reasons for feeling and thinking as you do. Talk openly about misunderstandings, and once you've shared mutually and there is at least some agreement, move on.

Further to this, these are some methods you can use for better teamwork as a couple:

- Use the words "I feel" to focus on your feelings and not blame the other.

- Repeat what you say. Say it again in different words; it helps your partner's mind not to wander. Also, repeat back to him or her what your partner says.

- Talk in a comfortable, un-distracting place and communicate face to face so you see each other's expressions.

- Your partner must try to maintain eye contact when listening to you. It's actually very difficult for some ADHD sufferers and non-neurotypical people to do. When they must talk to you, it's even harder. What they can do is to look at your face as a whole, or look at your nose instead.

- Some people find chewing gum and squeeze balls help them concentrate on a conversation. So if your partner does this, don't let that irritate you – it could be helpful.

- It is perfectly all right to divide up common chores and duties according to what you are better at; so your partner can concentrate on what he or she finds easier, or is better at than you are. Delegate jobs. In that way, you can get things done without stress or feeling overworked;

- Ask questions of each other; don't be ashamed.

- Afterwards, write down some important conclusions or information from the conversation, such as how you are going to co-operate, etc.

- He or she needs to talk about how ADHD makes organizing life and remembering difficult. Sharing their battles will help you to stand in their shoes and understand their behavior.

- Evaluate your work. After a week or so, meet and evaluate how your schedules are and if some situation or other has changed. Look back over the period. Decide if you are happy with an arrangement or not.

- Lastly, plan time to be together just for the sake of being together; decide when you are going to have fun! Life isn't just about solving problems.

If you've read through all this advice, it may help you to see what it would look like in practice. I will use the fictional examples of Janine and Chris to illustrate.

What could Janine do to manage her time? She and Juan could agree to meet days before the party and agree to the following: In future, Janine mustn't try to make the birthday cake. It's too complicated, and she can't concentrate on other things. She must plan to buy the next birthday cake – not Juan. She must phone to order it, and collect it on the day. When she goes to collect it, she needs to resist the urge to use the outing in the car to get as many things done as possible. The other purchases can be made on another outing to the shops. Janine would benefit from a family organizer put up in an open area where they can all see it, and where she can put lists of purchases to make for herself and for Juan. If Bella wants to help her, say that she's welcome to come half an hour before, to help with the last preparations, and the party itself.

When Janine can say she did the catering, that she chose and planned to buy the cake rather than make it, when Juan was able to stay with the games in the garden and the welcoming of each little boy and girl at the gate, greeting each parent or guardian (as was always his job) then she can say she was successful. She achieved her goal of organizing her daughter Sylvie's party. After the party, they need to talk again and ask themselves how it went, what was a problem, and what successes they can celebrate. If she really wants to practice making a cake, the best time to do it is on no special occasion: just something to have with coffee in the afternoon. She can give herself time then, without becoming stressed about deadlines.

In the case of Chris, Savannah could tell him that she's going to put a basket in his office space for tools. It's going to be beside his desk: all drill-bits, screws, samples of wood and anything not related to an office must go in there. She must agree not to put the things in there herself. Why not set up a cork-board to pin reminders on, in bright colors? Savannah would do well to let Chris show her what's on the hard drive of his computer. She could suggest that he sort his e-mail communication into four folders: his existing inbox for unread mail only; then make another folder for general communications he has read, or work he hasn't decided on yet; then divide his clients into two types with a folder each (small Jobs and large Jobs). Savannah must let HIM sort out his backlog of e-mails into these four places. However, as he goes through the backlog, he is sure to come across things he's forgotten. When he does, he must control his attention, so he can write reminders on colored notes for the cork-board, but he must carry on with the basic sorting, and finish it!

Maybe she can ask him a couple of weeks later how the computer is helping him organize his life. They can meet just to talk about the organizing, and be open about how they feel it's working, or not. Savannah needs to let Chris show her his computer organizing, but resist the urge firmly to do all the work for him.

Final Thoughts on Managing ADHD in a Relationship

Some of this advice is certain to be very helpful to you and your spouse or partner. It looks rather complicated if viewed up close, doesn't it? Keep your own focus by reminding yourself that it's about basically helping him or her do what he or she needs to do, but not doing it all yourself.

My last point here is to acknowledge to you that it's not going to be easy. I never said that it would be – but I assure you that improving your relationship is possible when the two of you accept the challenge and agree, in love, to face it.

CHAPTER 6: SEEKING HELP

ADHD is a huge burden for anyone who suffers from it. Whether your spouse or partner has had the diagnosis for some time, or has just recently found out about it, it makes sense to get professional help and to contact fellow victims. Even if you only suspect your partner suffers from ADHD, the answer is to get a professional opinion. Both you and your partner can get so much assistance; and both of you need not just to survive, but to thrive in your relationship.

What about the partner who doesn't want to go for evaluation, or who's been diagnosed and refuses to accept that outside help is needed? Some resistance to the idea of going to a so-called "institution" is understandable, given the average victim's experience of the institutions of school and home. It sort of conjures up images of the headteacher's office at school; of disappointed parents sending little Johnnie to a "shrink" because he's always in trouble, and the school's patience is running out; of Linda's mother going to the doctor and suggesting that her daughter needs a tranquilizer because Linda's hyper-sensitive, and some-times explodes into shouting matches with Mom.

I want to motivate you to do all you can, in the right tone, to persuade your partner to get some kind of professional advice and help. So many undiagnosed victims battle in their self-learnt coping strategies that might include drink or sleeping tablets, or just a frantic attempt to do things the way neurotypical people do, even though that way will rarely work for an ADHD vic-tim. Others just resign themselves to being supposedly "lazy" or unsuccessful.

If you or someone else doesn't succeed in persuading him or her to get help, I can still say that the advice in this book will be very useful. That's because it is, after all, written for you, the non-ADHD partner in your relationship. At least YOU know what's happening, and what to do, and not to do, from your side of the equation. So if your conversations stagnate or turn into arguments, don't despair; be patient and leave it for another day or month. You can work on many ways to help yourself and your partner in the meantime.

I am also very aware that not everyone lives in a wealthy, West-ern country, and has the possibility of affordable professional advice. Even people in affluent countries don't always have the services there whenever needed. They often must wait, and paid help can be expensive. In such cases, you will want to get whatever help you can, and the advice in this chapter is designed to assist.

Please be aware that the advice given in this book is not an official diagnosis. To get qualified advice and treatment, you will have to use the services of a professional medical and, or, psychological practitioner.

Medical Help – Drugs That Treat ADHD

Medicine to help ADHD has changed the lives of many sufferers. There is an important place for medication in the treatment of those with ADHD, and this definitely includes adults.

The first thing a psychiatrist or a doctor will do is make a diagnosis. Is it ADHD? This is really important, because ADHD can cause or worsen other neurological problems, and the treatment also needs to take into account whether someone is already being treated for other conditions.

The latest guidelines state that some ADHD-type symptoms must have been visible in a patient's life before the age of 12. He or she must find life significantly difficult, and the symptoms must have continued for six months or more.

All ADHD drugs work on the chemicals in the brain, known as neurotransmitters. These are dopamine and norepinephrine. Most drugs increase the levels of both these substances in the connections of the human brain, but others increase only the norepinephrine.

There are two basic types of ADHD drugs: stimulants and non-stimulants.

Stimulant drugs used in treating ADHD are types of amphetamines and methylphenidates. These substances increase the levels dopamine and norepinephrine. At the same time, both types of drugs slow down the effect of monoamine oxidase, which is an enzyme that breaks down neurotransmitters.

Non-stimulant drugs used in treating ADHD include atomoxetine (usually branded as Strattera), which works by increasing levels of norepinephrine only; tricyclic antidepressants, and bupropion (usually branded as Wellbutrin). Tricyclic antidepressants also affect levels of norepinephrine only, whereas bupropion affects levels of both norepinephrine and dopamine.

We can also divide drugs into categories depending on how long they work for. Short-acting stimulant drugs usually last for four to five hours. They must usually be taken two to three times a day. Long-acting drugs have an effect from six to eight hours, or even more than 12 hours. Finally, atomoxetine (Strattera) works at the required level for about 24 hours and can be taken once daily.

Generally speaking, stimulants are more effective and work more quickly than non-stimulants – as fast as an hour or two after dosage. Atomoxetine takes a couple of weeks to achieve noticeable effects, and up to 6 to 8 weeks before maximum effectiveness.

Unfortunately, stimulants can become addictive, and an ADHD patient might already be affected by abusing other stimulant drugs, non-medically, beforehand. Alcohol use can also have an impact on medication. Non-stimulant ADHD prescription drugs are not likely to be abused. There are also possible side-effects of neurological drugs, some mild and common, others serious. Certain illnesses and other medications might make it inadvisable or impossible for a doctor or psychiatrist to prescribe certain ADHD medications.

This being the case, when your partner sees a professional, the doctor or psychiatrist should know his or her medical history in detail. What medical conditions does he or she suffer from? And in the past? What medication is your spouse or partner using at that moment? Does he or she have allergies, especially to some medications? Is she pregnant, likely to be, or still breastfeeding? A professional must know all this and be reasonably certain that it's a case of ADHD, before your partner starts taking any medication.

I am not criticizing medication. Any reading of a support group website will show you dozens of people who say their lives have been turned around since they started using ADHD-specific drugs. They describe how they start to think clearly, how the world takes on a new feel, and remembering things becomes easier. Some, who were exhausted most of the time, find the energy to start doing the things that were put off, or they could never finish. Others who screamed around because they couldn't sit still for a minute, start to concentrate and feel calmer. Yes, medication really helps some adults. But I have to keep using the word "some" because ADHD can vary so much from person to person.

My cautious recommendation of "meds" is just to make clear it's not your partner's cure; it's a help. The medication may need to be taken for the rest of his or her life, or may have to be changed or discontinued in ill health and old age. I just want to be realistic. Medication is not magic, but when combined with guided learning, overcoming all the negative attitudes of other people that were internalized, and finding his or her best way to live, it's a great help.

Dosage and timing are important skills to learn. Does someone want to dose himself at breakfast with medication that will only take effect after he has driven to work? Perhaps he will drive and concentrate so much more safely, and with less stress, if he takes the meds as soon as he gets up. If someone else takes tablets three times a day, are the easiest times of day to take them too close together – so that she's left with an evening gap where tiredness and forgetting things will return? Setting an alarm for a certain time, and having reminders from you, can help your spouse or partner avoid these periods of reduced effect.

If any neurological condition is being treated with medicine, and your spouse doesn't feel happy with the effects, talk to the doctor who prescribed it, or if not possible, to another medical professional. You can't just decide you don't want it anymore, and stop suddenly. There is a risk of unpleasant or even dangerous reactions if this occurs.

Sometimes professionals put patients on a preliminary trial of a drug, with a beginning dosage, middle dosage and tapered end. Then he or she will evaluate that patient medically and by interview. This may be in your partner's best interests, since there is a wide choice of medications, and not all of them work well for a given individual.

Some drugs can reduce in effectiveness over time as the human body adapts to them; or many years of treatment might have long-term effects. In the past, doctors in some countries were over-prescribing anti-depressants and other psychiatric medications (although not as much in the case of specific ADHD medicine). Some patients were able to stop feeling depressed and lethargic, but ended up with what seemed like hyperactive

ADHD symptoms, and on top of that, paranoid feelings that their families and the doctor were against them. Paranoia is not a usual symptom of ADHD.

I don't want to put anyone off. There is an important, sure and vital way to avoid these experiences. You are one of them. You must become involved. Family, partners and close friends need to be involved to help both patient and doctor evaluate the effects. You are the ones who can notice small but important improvements or unwanted side-effects that could be difficult for your partner to see. You can just be supportive, and give him or her confirmation of what they are feeling. You are the ones who, hopefully, understand the ADHD patient's needs. You can also be the one to help your spouse or partner avoid the negative, "cancerous" effects of unsympathetic family members. The ones who declare that your partner mustn't use ADHD as an excuse to be lazy, or to feel sorry for him- or herself...

Psychological Help – Counseling and Skills That Help ADHD

Are medicines enough for someone who suffers from ADHD? No, I don't believe they are enough. Sufferers still need to learn skills to think and organize, and to strengthen and heal their relationships with other people.

Again, I am telling you what so many partners of people with ADHD, and so many victims of the condition, too, are saying: counseling and understanding, learning better strategies and getting help from support groups, and so on, make a great difference to their lives.

You see, when someone has grown up trying to do things but not knowing why they work badly, or becomes resigned to failure, they need to change their thinking. That's not a criticism of those who live with ADHD: it should be an enormous relief. Drugs can't think for you, however. The ways to get daily life to work for your partner and for you will be different for different couples, because of the highly variable nature of ADHD. He or she needs to find what works for them as an individual, and to learn what was too difficult to learn in earlier life. This is the case for everyone who has ADHD.

Again, your involvement is essential to help your partner.

In the previous chapter, I went through lists of helpful methods and tips for living. There are so many that it can look really confusing, especially to someone battling to concentrate because of ADHD. Therapy and professional help enable someone to step back and look at the bigger picture. Your partner needs to ask: What do I actually need to put right, and what are the underlying strategies I am going to use to do so? Those are the deeper questions – really important, but simple.

There are several kinds of therapies for ADHD. Some practitioners combine them, others specialize in one only. They include psychodynamic therapy, behavioral therapy, CBT (cognitive behavioral therapy), and humanistic or philosophical therapy.

Psychodynamic therapy is done by working through your thoughts and patterns of behavior that are the result of unconscious fear and past experiences, especially traumatic ones, with the guidance of your therapist. Your partner, as the client, would work with him or her to identify these damaging thoughts and find out what impact they've been making; and then seek to replace them with more conscious and adult thought patterns. The therapist will analyze your spouse or partner's emotions and will look at relationships "then" and "now."

Behavioral therapy is focused on your actual behavior when it isn't adaptive or helpful. Unconscious reasons are not so important: instead, the client learns relaxation techniques and ways to face unpleasant situations. One might be deliberately exposed to stressful situations with the help of a therapist's presence, and learn to handle them; or have "aversion therapy" where undesirable, unhelpful behavior such as binge drinking is associated with some unpleasant thought or stimulus and so becomes less appealing.

Cognitive Behavioral Therapy (CBT) focuses not so much on actual behaviors as on unhelpful, conscious thought patterns, inner dialogues, or negative beliefs. These could be having a stressful, negative impact on the situations your partner must face. They might lead to serious depression or mood swings, which only make organizing life harder.

The good thing about CBT is that it can be done as a couple, an individual, or in a group. People with ADHD are often very self-critical because of the way they seemed to fail, as children, at tasks others did well in. This might affect their mental well-being through life; however, CBT can help people to talk to themselves more positively, as well as teaching them how to improve their focus and their time-management skills.

Clients of a CBT practitioner might keep a diary of their negative thoughts and positive ones, practicing how to replace negative beliefs with more rational inner dialogue. They also learn "emotional awareness": how to identify their emotions and understand what they actually feel, and then regulate them, being able to reject sensations when they are inappropriate or irrational. Other emotions they will learn to accept as normal and allow themselves to feel.

Humanistic, or existential, therapy is an approach where the client is invited to look at how his or her view of the world affects daily life. It has the basis that each one of us is the best person to understand what we feel and experience, and that we need to be who we were truly meant to be. Therapists and counselors using this method usually try to show you unconditional respect and acceptance, helping you make decisions without being forced by their judgement, or anyone else's. The philosophy is one of self-acceptance. Some practitioners approach their work from a religious point of view, helping their clients to face their challenges in the awareness of God and of the ultimate meaning and value of their existence, despite its challenges. Others focus on personal growth against the background of interpersonal relationships which give meaning to human life.

Your partner would share and evaluate his or her decisions in life. The therapist may ask questions to help him or her to understand, but the client, your partner, will be the one to make the decisions. Personal growth is always one of the goals of humanistic therapy. Where other people have criticized or otherwise discouraged your partner, their disapproval makes self-acceptance difficult. With empathy and reflection, he or she can dare to grow and challenge these ignorant opinions, and find his or her best way to live.

Other aspects of humanistic therapy look at unresolved issues like family relationship problems and other conflicts. You and your partner can also examine your relationship in all of the aspects I mentioned, learning how to have empathy and understanding of each other, and to respect each other's point of view and personal experiences. Some practitioners use role-playing or acting to help their clients manage their relationships and understand other people's points of view.

There are some practical aspects of looking after yourself that all of us need, and ADHD sufferers even more so. To help your partner, a therapist might get him or her to recognize the effects of tiredness and overwork. It's often very draining for someone with ADHD to do a day's or night's work, and sleep is difficult for many of them. Some guidelines and advice here, or a review of recent patterns, can help your partner to get enough rest. Eating properly is also an aspect of life that some victims struggle to achieve, and need advice about. Nutrition is important for managing ADHD but there is no need to be obsessive about it. Previously, it was thought that sugary foods and certain refined substances were the culprits, but this has not been proven. It is possible that taking Omega-3 oils can help, and eating a high-protein diet with fresh foods included, and enough slow-digesting carbohydrates, seems to help sufferers just to be healthier – and so to manage life because they feel better. There are many other tips to help your partner eat well.

Social and Community Help – Support Groups and Websites

Even with an amazing amount of support from you, and a loving commitment from your partner to overcome his or her challenges , it can still feel as if the two of you are in a small boat, sailing in a vast ocean. Nothing could be further from the truth. ADHD is not rare. Why not contact other like-minded people, other victims of this disorder – and their spouses and partners who are in the same boat as you?

Support groups are usually free; if you can find a nearby group where you can have face-to-face, that will be better. However, the wonderful thing is that there are also groups online, with members all over the world. If you live in an isolated area, a foreign country, or simply don't have anything nearby, there is no need to worry because you can still be part of a forum, or even a video-conference group.

Some groups are coordinated by a licensed therapist or coach, others just directed by their members. Your partner can speak to other people who have to tackle the same kind of challenges that he or she does. Recently-diagnosed members can learn from those who have handled their condition with understanding for a long time, finding out what to do and what not to. You can get advice and practical tips to help both of you manage.

You would also do well to find a support group just for spouses and partners of people with ADHD. You can vent your frustrations without losing respect for your partner – because you will know that those who hear you understand your situation. It's theirs, too.

All of this is to help you to understand your partner and overcome negative feelings, or identify where he or she isn't cooperating. This, and related topics, will be covered in the following chapters.

PART 3 - TRULY LOVE SOMEONE WITH ADHD

CHAPTER 7: FACING THE DIFFICULTIES OF LOVING SOMEONE WITH ADHD

The wide-ranging and lifelong effects of ADHD in one partner put a lot of strain on any relationship. The rate of divorce in such circumstances is higher than for two non-ADHD sufferers, and we can understand why. Nevertheless, I want to encourage those of you who are committed to staying together, making things work, and learning new and better strategies for living. It is possible to be happy together when there is goodwill and patience. You don't have to be a statistic.

It helps to go through some of the challenges and look at them squarely, though. First of all, there are the ways that intimacy in general, sexual intercourse included, are damaged or frustrated by the ADHD symptoms of one partner.

Problems with Intimacy and Sex

Distraction and its opposite, hyper-focusing, can strain a relationship. Intimacy needs regular effort and frequent attention to be maintained, and a few surprising and interesting little romantic gestures help to keep it up. But the non-ADHD partner might get no attention at all for some time, because his or her partner is caught up with some other interest or worry. Then later, he or she might get floods of attention, maybe lots of sex to the point of excess. A sort of bouncing between extremes, and it's not romantic.

Someone who suffers from ADHD is often restless and tired, and seeks some kind of new interest or escape. Routine and regular conversation or a quiet "sundowner" drink on the porch might become boring. You may feel as if he or she is just there out of habit, that you aren't being listened to. Maybe your partner rushes off when she sees the ripe fruit on your trees in the orchard, and starts picking them, just leaving you there.

The 24-hour television and then the mobile telephone are some of the most powerful distractions in our lives. In one generation they've multiplied the information we can get access to, as well as multiplied the need to separate, organize and control it – all things your partner has problems with. Why, once the TV sat in the lounge; now we've brought it into the bedroom! So we really can have "three in a bed." If you are both watching it, you aren't really talking to one another. You can become excited, angered and shocked by what you see – instead of being comforted, attracted and aroused by each other.

Some non-ADHD partners get the feeling, quite rightly, that sex is becoming dull and uninteresting for their partner. When that happens, some people jump to the conclusion that their husband, wife, or other partner is having an affair, when this is not the case. However, the boredom and distraction they notice is real, and it's a problem. Though it's not necessarily a sign that they don't love any more, it is a signal that they aren't able to keep focused on you. Then there are people with ADHD who do go off and have affairs; more on that later.

Trauma in childhood has tremendous negative consequences for loving and bonding as an adult. Growing up with the symptoms of ADHD resulted for many in criticism, harsh punishment and peer rejection. As I covered earlier, their self-esteem is damaged, so the victim feels shame and unworthiness.

The effect of this is that a victim feels abnormal and without value, and he or she goes on to develop shyness and social anxiety. When you feel like that, you are far less likely to learn how to date, to tell someone that he or she's attractive, to decide whether you want to accept or refuse someone else's declaration that they are attracted to you. As a teen, this is a set of skills you learn for adult life. Many ADHD victims haven't learnt these skills, or are inexperienced and unconfident with them.

Then, in adult life, they may avoid or lack confidence in emotional and sexual intimacy, despite feeling the need for it in some way, and having married or at least started a sexual relationship. In violent contrast, other people are drawn to obsessive-compulsive sexual behavior such as pornography, or having affairs when their marriage or stable relationship becomes strained.

This can create, for such people, what some psychologists call a "love-lust conflict." Many neurotypical people feel both love and lust for a person they love; their emotional expression and their sexual satisfaction come together. Men often voice a concern, or simply admit, that they feel lust outside of a love relationship as well, and most of these men aren't suffering from ADHD. However, it's important to realize that they definitely do, or at least did at one point, feel both sexual and emotional attraction for their partners. They may be dissatisfied with their sexual relationship and want, or have, sex outside the relationship and thus damage it further. However, it usually means that they are also seeking emotional attraction from the woman they are having an affair with.

In contrast, many people who have suffered psychological trauma can't seem to combine the two attractions. They can love someone, but don't seem to be able to keep, or attain, feelings of sexual attraction. ADHD victims seem to be prone to this state of emotions. Some theorists say that this is because they are taught in various ways as children that sex is "bad," but love is "good." Our popular culture seems to collaborate in this distortion: you see the words, "naughty pleasures," "forbidden lusts," "XXX films," and so on. Thus, they grow up to feel aroused by what is "bad." Have they been taught, unconsciously, that a long-term, committed relationship is "boring?"

One consequence of this is using pornography. ADHD people need stimulation, and in porn, there it is. Problem-causing porn, used individually and secretly by your partner, makes you, the non-ADHD partner, feel inadequate and ignored. You might even open up and say so, or try lovingly to ask, "Why am I not good enough? What do I need to do, or not do? Why can't you tell me instead of sneaking in porn?" You do need to talk about it, but you risk getting a defensive, shamed reaction. I'm not turning a blind eye to this problem, but I'm just saying clearly that shaming isn't a solution. It actually makes the itch for excitement and escape worse. Most of this explanation is aimed at female partners of ADHD-affected men, but in the case of a female partner found looking at porn alone, her male husband or partner may react with even greater disgust, shaming her yet more forcefully. Society has less tolerance for women and porn.

It goes without saying that porn can turn into a serious, time-grabbing obsession that sometimes causes its victims to lose their jobs, isolate themselves, or spend all their money. That's a relationship killer.

Affairs are even more of a relationship killer. They can happen in an oddly similar way to your partner's other, less shaming, thrill-seeking activities such as extreme sports, racing and even just changing jobs out of frustration and boredom. Left unchallenged and uncounseled, an ADHD victim who's had one affair may do it again and again. Communication and openness are going to be required to heal this damage; openness about your partner's very personal inner pain and rejection. As I say, I don't justify your partner's bad behavior, but I do want you to understand what drives it.

Most importantly, if you also tend to feel low self-esteem, don't blame yourself for these problems in your partner's life! It's not what you have or haven't done, and not because you "aren't good enough," "aren't young enough," or whatever. The problem is your partner's, but it needs to be identified and understood in order to be solved.

I think it's relevant here to mention the case of a partner who is watching same-sex porn, or is found to be having a relationship with someone of the same sex, in secret. The same consideration applies here. You two need to talk about it, perhaps with the aid of a counselor or other therapist. Hiding things in shame isn't going to help you or your partner. There's something you need to accept here; maybe not justify, but acknowledge. Importantly, in this case it cannot be true by definition that, "I'm not a good enough woman for him/I'm not a good enough man for her," so don't say this kind of thing and blame yourself. The problem is a need in your partner, and he or she needs to understand it, as you do.

It may be an important indication that your partner never really felt physical attraction for you –that may not be the case at all: don't jump to conclusions. There is no law of human nature that makes all people attracted either to the opposite, or the same sex. Thinking there is belies a sort of false dichotomy or division. However, a partner who is looking for "forbidden" thrills and who has sex with various people of the same sex, has a problem which needs serious attention before it wrecks your relationship. The same goes for "forbidden" thrills with people of the opposite sex. But a partner who has a deep need for friendship of an intense kind with someone of the same sex is a different case, a case of someone who may still care about you and find you attractive. ADHD makes caring and attraction harder to see in moments of your partner's escapism and stress. That is an extra challenge in an already challenging situation.

"Parent-Child" Communication Is Bad for Both of You

In Chapter Five, I looked at the "Parent-Child" style of communication which often develops in relationships with someone who has ADHD. It damages the essential equality there ought to be between partners in any romantic relationship. You may, as I pointed out, be trying to help in a nurturing way, but you are taking on more responsibility than your partner is.

People with ADHD or any other problem may resent your taking over, e.g. in matters of money. If you are the partner who earns more, or all of the money in the household, he or she may become grudging and negative even if you ask his or her opinion about some expense. You might hear, "Well, it's your money, so why bother asking what I think you should do with it?" If your partner is the main or sole earner, this problem can still occur when he or she feels left out, or used: "It seems I'm good enough to earn it, but not good enough to decide what to do with it!"

The opposite is also true – the partner with ADHD may behave passively, and just not bother to do anything, or help. Or, they might behave irresponsibly and immaturely. Some relationships drift one way, some the opposite way. Others drift in different directions at different times. In cases where the partner with ADHD seems to acquiesce and agree to the "parenting" by the other, he or she can still hide a lot of hidden resentment, because they know that you are not an actual parent, and he or she isn't a child.

Another challenge to consider in this dynamic is that the non-ADHD partner can feel un-thanked and used. The work of being a "Parent," especially a nurturing "Parent," is hard work, the kind that normally brings a reward or a thanks. If your partner resents the way you take over, correct, and plan everything (by implication saying that he or she is no good at doing anything), then you probably won't get any thanks. Or, if he or she accepts the dynamic hopelessly, the thanks will be rather weak and rather forced. Is that what you really want?

Lastly, the challenge of this dynamic is the sheer weight of the responsibility. In the worst of scenarios, you may find your partner in trouble with the law over drunkenness and driving, drug-use, or a violent argument in public. Less obviously, you will condemn yourself to years of straining to manage your life and your partner's at the same time.

With all that said, it's very hard not to fall into the trap of the "Parent-Child" dynamic. You will need to find ways to support your partner that involve consciously not being a pseudo-"Parent," and willingly allowing him or her to have responsibility. This I will cover in the next chapter.

Other Points of Challenge

One of the symptoms of ADHD is having poor control of impulses and emotions, and a consequence of that, in turn, is getting into arguments and stirring up opposition. What begins as unintentional provocation can end up becoming a habit. Victims may feel tempted to vent their frustration and anger by aggravating and even causing conflict.

You may have to witness and live through your partner's conflicts. Perhaps you're a natural peacemaker: acting as a "Parent" again, you may try to help your beloved solve their issues. You might just achieve it – at the price of great strain and emotional draining. Perhaps you will fail, and then suffer even more.

It goes without saying that your own conversation and interaction can turn conflictive and argumentative. If you are an emotionally expressive person, you may find that you aggravate your partner, and/or, he or she aggravates you. There are no winners when you're both fighting.

Another consequence of impulsivity is acting before thinking of the consequences. That might not lead to a fight, but it's likely to lead to many failures and regrets. What happens then? It sets up an insidious pattern of failure, and self-defeating expectations. Imagine it from your partner's point of view: every time you get an inspiration, you rush off excitedly and try to act on it, but the result is failure. Soon, you come to believe you are a failure, and stop trying to follow your goals and desires. As the long-suffering girlfriend, boyfriend, or spouse of someone with ADHD, you will have to deal with their depressed state that results. A pertinent example is when your partner loses a job – something ADHD-sufferers are very prone to doing (the statistics show a far higher rate of unemployment among those diagnosed with ADHD). If his or her attempts to find work are unrealistic or poorly planned, he or she may become depressed and stop trying to find work.

Sufferers who are hyperactive and impulsive, and who won't slow down, are a huge challenge to people who love them, simply because of the energy it takes to keep up with them. You may be a very different kind of person – calm and outwardly tranquil. If it is true that opposites attract, that may have been the reason you were drawn to one another in the first place. However, it can become a point of conflict when you just don't have the energy to accompany them, and remember all they are trying to do (which they're going to forget half of, anyway). You may be fearing the impending waste or failure of their present flurry of activity, or your having to help your partner to finish it. He or she may think you don't care about what they do, and assume falsely that you don't think it's good enough.

The Serious Behavioral Problems

I have mentioned these before, however, it has to be repeated that one of the greatest challenges of life with some ADHD sufferers is putting up with dangerous or anti-social behavior. This may include recreational drug use, dangerous sports or risky driving, serious and violent depression, suicidal behavior, and physical violence toward others, especially spouses and partners. You may have been hit or slapped; or emotionally, or sexually abused, by someone with serious ADHD problems.

Most people who live with ADHD don't get into such trouble. Yet some do, and the results can be serious enough to threaten not only your well-being but your safety, and put you in serious need of help.

Self-Care

This is one of the most unrecognized challenges of being the partner of someone with ADHD. The strain takes its toll on you, and you yourself need to take time just for you. It's easy to focus so much on your partner and what he or she needs, does, and doesn't do, that you forget to look after yourself. It's a subtle consequence of the insidious "Parent-Child" dynamic – parents look after children, not the other way around (until we're very old). You can end up with serious psychological problems of your own, or your existing weaknesses and challenges become worse – after all, who's without their own weaknesses and handicaps?

A diagnosis of ADHD can take away some stress, while you accept the reality of it in your shared situation, but a sort of "ADHD-ghost", as I call it, sometimes takes over in a relationship. It's where ADHD thoughts and awareness seem to dominate every moment and each conversation. It seems to influence and control everything, and everyone in your family. You need to take time out for yourself: you may be drifting apart from friends, ignoring hobbies and anything that simply isn't ADHD related.

You need to find and keep your own happiness. To be happy is not to be selfish: you truly need happiness in order to make others happy. So one challenge you must face is not to let the situation stop you from doing activities, or spending times with people, that make you happy. You might realize suddenly that you hardly ever laugh. If so, you need to put this right!

If your partner is violent or similarly abusive, you must never allow yourself to accept such treatment. I make many excuses for ADHD sufferers, but there is a lot of their behavior that I cannot help but condemn. They aren't bad people by definition; they're simply humans with ADHD, but that doesn't make them all innocent victims. Some of them can and do abuse others to make up for their feelings of lack of control, or the pain of criticism, or of damaged self-esteem. In such cases you need help – legal and police help included. The last chapters of this book will deal more specifically with this and other aspects of a relationship which has ended, or is in serious danger, because of abusive actions and behavior.

In the next chapter, and with an eye to remembering some of the tips I covered in the previous chapter, I want to show you some more ways to support your partner, avoid the "Parent-Child" dynamic, really help him or her, and get the balance right.

CHAPTER 8: ASSISTING YOUR PARTNER

Supporting your partner in the right way means sharing but not taking over; understanding and communicating with him or her instead of announcing rules and procedures, and not doing things without your partner's knowledge so that they find out only later. To lay the groundwork for that, and to stop thinking in a false, "Parent-Child" sort of way, you need to realize that you could be hiding a lot of negative emotion towards them. Understandable but unhelpful, this sort of anger and frustration doesn't help you to deal with your spouse or partner's problematic behavior, or to heal the damage to your relationship.

Such emotions are likely to rise into your consciousness when you argue, or when he or she does or says something that triggers a sudden reaction in you. What can help you?

Overcoming Negative Emotions Towards Your Partner

There's a very effective way for you to overcome those negative, frustrated emotions when you and your partner disagree, or meet some obstacle.

Stand in your partner's shoes.

It's easier said than done. One way to do it is to go to the source of help which I've mentioned previously: online groups and forums.

Read the comments and contributions by ADHD sufferers, and you will take a look into their struggles, and into their minds. Imagine that you are your partner. Now consider these situations...

- Imagine that you finally get a diagnosis of ADHD as an adult, after years of battling symptoms. When you tell your parents, hoping for some shared understanding, they say glibly that they knew about it. When you were small, the family GP doctor told them that you probably had it, but they just brushed his advice off because: "Everyone knows that's not a real disease."

- What if you had to try six or seven different medications before you found the right drug for you? Some might just not work, others might give you nausea or make you too agitated, or sleepy. Some people might feel suddenly paranoid, fearing unreasonably that they're going to have an accident. Is that because of the "meds?" You'll have to talk about this to the practitioner who prescribed them. Maybe you're just worrying too much? Maybe you've noticed an important warning sign.

- You have problems with your memory. You forget to go to the clinic to pick up your next prescription. So you run out of medication, and feel awful, confused and unmotivated. You have to put a couple of pills in an extra container so you have an extra day's supply, if you can't or don't go to collect them on the day.

- What does it feel like to pick up your medication at a pharmacy where you have to rub shoulders with drug addicts and methadone users trying to get off the hard stuff? When the personnel (who don't know you are an ADHD sufferer) treat you like something dirty and crazy, an unwanted social cost instead of a customer?

- Imagine you take "meds" for a couple of years and they help you so much. Then your new doctor just decides that you "don't have ADHD" and stops the prescription.

- What do you feel, living in a Western country where ADHD is diagnosed quite often, when you hear people saying to you, "Oh, but my cousin has ADHD and he's got a really good job." (You don't.) Or, "Oh, but my friend's daughter has ADHD, and she's never had a car accident." (You have.) Or else, "Oh, that's strange. I thought people usually grow out of it by the time they're in their teens." (You haven't. Actually, as you read this book you will understand that I believe anyone grows out of ADHD. They might be handling it better – or hiding and masking it more; this book is to help you do the first, and not the second.)

- What does it feel like being someone who has ADHD and manages to do some things well? Some people keep their jobs, get good marks when they study, and bring up their children, yes... but... Over and over again such sufferers say, "It comes with a terrible price." Imagine: you arrive home exhausted. You eat junk because you can't even think about cooking. Or, you're single because your partner left you, and there's no-one to help you. You can't find anything at home. Or, you hardly ever clean your house, and your partner slams you for being "dirty," saying that if you can do your job/study/look after the kids, why can't you do that as well? You say it's because you have no energy left. You can't remember where the cleaning materials are. You forget to do half of the corridor. Then everyone reminds you that so-and-so has five children and is studying online, and her house is beautifully organized. That he works 40 hours a week, and still turns out vast numbers of wooden items as a hobby, and goes to all his kids' sports matches...

- What about the person whose ADHD is so serious that they can't work? When they literally turn on the television and are still there six hours later? When they feel constant pain, dullness and confusion? When they just don't have the motivation to even walk outside? When their partner comes home and finds they haven't washed the dishes? "Couldn't you even do at least that?" Yes, you could... and what about the rest of the day, and the rest of your life?

- Imagine that you really wanted to have a career in scientific research, and you got good enough grades at school after a terrible struggle, but you gave up the thought and work packing supermarket shelves (and have had a hundred similar jobs over time). You gave up because you thought you'd never be able to handle the pressure.

- Imagine you have a fairly long conversation with someone you know; they talk a lot and then ask you why you aren't commenting. You realize that your responses were all in your mind – without being aware, you actually sat in complete silence.

- Can you imagine what life is like when you talk to someone and explain things to them, but cannot get rid of a terrible feeling that they don't understand you? So you feel that you have to give more and more details, to make them visualize what you say? Then they tell you that you talk too much, or that you treat them like a fool.

- What's it like to sit, frozen with fear, thinking about all the things you have to do, for hours, because you cannot decide where to begin?

- What is it like to keep running all the time? Perhaps physically, always mentally. The moment you sit down, you start to fidget. You scratch your face, pick your nails. You don't want to spend a second thinking about your home, let alone your relationship, because you know they're in a mess. It's better to do something outside of it to dull the discomfort and pain. Maybe where there is loud music, and in discotheques, you finally feel happy and relaxed – for an hour or two – before restlessness comes back.

- What is life like when you've never slept through a

single night without waking up several times, or never fallen asleep more quickly than after an hour of getting to bed? Or what about when you sleep for twelve hours after you drink alcohol on an empty stomach, and get up feeling hungry, but can't find the strength to eat anything?

- What if the reason you collapsed at home was because you hadn't eaten for several days, even though there was food in the house?

- If you take the highest dose of an ADHD drug, and get only a slight improvement, how will that make you feel?

- What must it be like to live in a world of expectations that are already unreasonable? They keep pressuring you to do more and more, to handle your emotions better, to be friendly and people-centered but also assertive, to excel in a vast variety of daily tasks and chores, and to be visibly happy? People with ADHD can excel, but it costs them more!

- How do you fill in a CV/resumé with your work history when you've had over 50 jobs?

- What does it do to your self-image when you've been fired twenty times in your life?

- Can you imagine struggling for years to determine what people are thinking, when they don't express it clearly, but only by innuendo and clues? Then they accuse you of being "self-centered" when you don't guess correctly. What about when they tell you something important, but only in a few words, right in the middle of another conversation? Then you miss it completely, and they challenge you: "But I told you they were getting divorced..." You can't remember anything of it.

- Can you imagine twenty, or thirty, or forty years of people telling you to pay more attention? Or to try harder, when you were trying harder than almost everyone else in school, work, or wherever?

In any online group, there is no end of comments from people who pour out their frustrations, their depressions, and their anger from having to deal with life when they have ADHD. Perhaps one of the most compassionate things you can do to support your partner is to say, and mean it, that you don't expect them to do things like, or to be like other people. They have their own ways of thinking, and their own ways of achieving. You can give your spouse or partner encouragement to find ways that work for them.

Any support group, whether in person or online, is going to expose you and your partner to the struggles of others with

ADHD, and their partners' own hardships. Don't be ashamed to join one. Few people who seek help with others who are like-minded ever regret it.

I hope this led you to realize quite how bad life can be for your partner. Hopefully your frustration melts away, and you may feel indignant at the way he or she was, and is, being treated. Now to look at some more different and sometimes even enjoyable ways to help the two of you to improve your relationship and handle life better...

Areas Where Your Partner Will Need Help

- *Regulating his or her emotions.* When your partner can learn how to control emotions, express them without getting carried away, and not try to suppress them in silence, your relationship (and their interactions with everyone else) will be more peaceful. There are healthy ways to be aware of exactly what your emotions are, and what fear might be underlying your anger, for example. There are also better ways to express them. You could have a regular time each day, each week, or whatever, for your partner to share positive as well as negative feelings, and for you to do the same.

- *Knowing how to resolve conflict.* What is the style that the two of you have for negotiating, for trying to resolve a disagreement? There is a chance that your partner has gotten into the habit of being aggressive, hostile in his or her use of words, or of using personal remarks. Do you respond in kind? That's a recipe for unhappiness. He or she will have to learn to listen to you – and you to him or her. If you ask, "Why?" you must wait for and listen to the reply. There are other skills for communication that involve less aggressive words; the use of "I feel..." statements rather than "You always..." statements, for example.

- *Reaching goals and doing things together as a couple.* Your partner may find it hard to decide exactly what he or she wants to achieve with you. Do you? To stop him or her wasting time and energy, you need to help him or her to look at smaller, easier-to-identify steps on the way to reaching your desired end stage. That could be as simple as finishing the vegetable garden before renovating the bathroom, or something like her finishing a course so she can be qualified for the job she wants. Talk about how much progress you and they are making towards these goals.

- *Overcoming his or her negative beliefs.* Your encouragement is needed in this area because most people with ADHD hide a lot of negative beliefs about themselves, and are resigned to such beliefs. They are prone to thinking of themselves as failures, unstable and "incurable," excessively dependent on others to cope, shameful and untrustworthy. You need to step in quickly but lovingly if they fly into an impulsive chain of negative talk or action, or act as if they are useless. This will have to be done as encouragement – if you do this badly, it could seem like yet more hostile correction, one of the causes of their negative beliefs in the first place. Ask them if you can tell them what you think, and then make it encouraging. You might also suggest ways to act that will bolster their self-image.

- *Hyperactive sufferers need to learn to calm down and not act on their deep inner restlessness.* They will need help with regulating their daily activities, to space them out and to monitor their progress. You will have to do this with them, not for them. Meditation and relaxation techniques, videos, and music may help them slow down their daily life and manage their runaway thoughts.

Intimacy, Distance and Closeness, and Touch

One of the most important things to keep working on in any romantic relationship is intimacy. When I use the word, "intimacy" I am talking about sex, but also about much, much more.

When you and your partner have frequent arguments, or when correcting him or her becomes a habit – the "Parent-Child Syndrome" – then closeness, affection, and love expressed in small ways... dies. Supporting your partner with ADHD is aided so much by loving, simple communication, both in words and in touch. Like the sort of conversation where you can just share your thoughts on something that you noticed. It could be a sunset, a new supermarket, or an outlandish, strange, pedigreed dog you saw. A quick joke maybe, or a small word of appreciation. Or just a plan to have a meal together at home where there's no agenda, and no business to discuss. When you do get those couple-focused moments, resist the urge to bring up problems. Don't use opportunities better meant for family life and being a couple, as levers to get a point across. Moments when you have to plan, or to talk about problems, are necessary; but don't look for them – make them. At other times.

Think back to the beginning of your relationship, to the small incidents, touches, and little remarks that remind you of how it began. They were moments of intimacy – sharing yourself. Not for getting something done in the process, but for sharing: just because sharing is what human, personal life is for.

Granted, if you are reading this book, it's likely to be because your partner's ADHD has been causing problems for both of you. These problems can still prove the value of intimacy: ask yourself if the things he or she does that hurt you, the incidents whose memory makes you feel angry or sad, are not just precisely those sort of little moments, gone wrong. Strengthening and repairing that bond between you and your partner will happen gradually when you are both able to make up for these sore points with little, positive interactions. Now you understand the deeper issues and the basic problem of ADHD; but the way to solve them isn't a mammoth, five-year remodeling plan: it's a day-by-day effort in little things.

Helping other people, the two of you together, is not just a chore – it can be a relief. So, if your aunt lives alone and you have to buy shopping for her; if his parents are old and frail and he needs to fix their garage door because it's stuck down; these could be opportunities to do things as a team.

Too many of us say to our significant others that we have to do our private stuff, and go off reluctantly to do it. Yes, these chores can be onerous, but when you and your partner are together in it, there will be greater understanding between you. Just the drive on the way back from these helping missions can be an opportunity to share your relief that things worked out, that a relative is happy, or just moan quietly about how they aren't coping with their lives. It's another type of intimacy.

The simplest way to achieve and keep intimacy is physical: it's touch. If you remember just one thing from this part of the chapter, realize how calming, loving and relaxing a massage can be!

No, I'm not referring to a blaze of little scented candles with a fountain in the background, nor an acrobatic session where you wear black lace for him, or a Tarzan-style loincloth for her. Those have their place, if you like! But no – just a simple head and neck massage. An opportunity to give and receive a bit of calm, to focus on relaxing, or an opportunity to loosen tired muscles and sore points. Touching someone gives an opportunity to look, to feel and to see how he or she is, without words. To notice what makes your partner happy, or where pain is felt. You can actually free frozen joints and cure some headaches, once you've learnt your partner and the techniques better. Have your partner lean back slightly in an easy chair, or sit upright where you can stand behind and support their neck and head. There is often tension around the eyes, along the jaw, and around the ears. So much of our stress causes us to clench our jaw shut, so that the muscles of our neck, and around the ears, suffer. He or she can breathe in slowly from the nose, but with mouth open and jaw stretched, then breathe out through the mouth and relax the jaw. It looks weird, but can be magic to relieve a tension headache.

Some people will want a more active, stretching massage, or to work on their tight shoulders, or back. Sometimes massage hurts a bit, but soon gives way to relief of pain or swelling. A mini-massage of one's hands or feet makes far more difference than you would think. Hands and feet are some of the most important, most-used and most-strained parts of the human body. After a foot massage, some people say they sense that they're walking on air...

However, if you or your partner have any underlying health problems, you must check with a medical practitioner about what is all right, and what isn't. Some massage is very vigorous; that could be excellent, or it could be too violent and jerking to provide any benefit. Some massage is so gentle that you could use it even on someone who is gravely ill, and give comfort without any bad effects.

There are many videos, tutorials and books offering advice and suggestions to guide you here. Not only can you support your partner and make him or her feel good, but your partner can help you to feel more intimate and comforted by massaging you, when it's your turn. Your partner with ADHD has as much to gain from learning to touch and calm you with massage as you do from giving one to him or her.

No, this doesn't have to be for sex. Yes, it could be a wonderful way to get into the mood for making love. Or, done the other way around, it could be an amazing way to prolong the closeness and warm feelings that you get after intercourse. However, massage can be for any mood: for times of sickness when the last thing you can imagine doing is having sex. Or just snatching a few minutes of a busy day that will be so much better for a younger couple than trying frantically to fit in a "quickie."

Sex and frequency of sex are subjects of tension for many couples. What often happens first is that intimacy – emotional, verbal and physical (in the general way that includes massage) – suffers. Then, many men find that sex is the only intimacy left. However, they find their female partner saying that it's too rushed, too often, and too tiring. Many women ask for it because they want emotional closeness, but their male partner just does it to release his tension, and there seems to be no connectedness afterwards.

Massage and non-aroused touch are not just a substitute for more frequent sex, although they could be. They are a way of communicating what you want, and finding out what your partner wants, and why. In addition, when you can explain in words how you feel – if sex is not possible, has been disappointing, or is too much in a given moment – and then you can still offer a massage, you will be responding without pulling away. That's so important. To shun or pull away can be very hurtful for any spouse or partner, and to give an embrace and a massage instead can help a lot.

ADHD and the Sense of Touch

The previous advice could be for any couple. What about ADHD, though? Does it affect this dynamic at all, and if so, what can you do?

ADHD and some other neurological conditions do affect people's sense of touch. Some sufferers are very jumpy and nervy, and though they might like calm touch, God help you if they don't know it's coming! You could be shouted at, shrugged off coolly, or even lashed out at involuntarily, and hit. Others are very sluggish, and don't seem to warm up or react to being touched, but these are a minority.

ADHD makes organizing input from the mind and the senses harder. Some sufferers are extremely sensitive. They may feel irritated if their clothes weren't washed with fabric-softener; they might hate loud music and sudden or sharp noises, or they smell everything as overpowering, avoiding strong perfume in personal toiletries or household cleaners. Victims may taste certain food as cloying, sickly and over-flavored. Others hate flashing or bright lights (epileptics especially have been known to have problems here). It's called "sensory overload."

Sensory overload results in it being impossible to pay attention properly, while the stimulus is impossible to ignore. That combination is infuriating and literally, physically painful for them.

This reaction doesn't always happen, but is likely in some given circumstances – more so if the ADHD-affected partner is concentrating hard on something, hyper-focusing. For example, you might find her, or him, at the computer screen and put a hand on their shoulder – a normally nice, little intimate touch – and get a retort of, "No! Don't do that! I can't concentrate." You might come across him or her reading a book, engrossed in the information, and ask a question out of the blue. The partner jumps violently and spins around, snapping, "Hey! You gave me a fright." Some people fly into a rage if there's someone whistling nearby. It makes it impossible for them to speak to you, or even hear you. They describe the low-quality, blurred but high-pitched sound as excruciatingly painful, impossible to shut out.

This can be a bit infuriating, seemingly hypocritical to you. Sometimes it comes from a person who often interrupts you, shifts restlessly, drifts off, makes tapping and scratching noises, or on occasion bursts out very loudly and animatedly... but now you know why. It's the effect of ADHD on concentration, and it's real.

What is the solution, with regard to physical intimacy? You could sum it up in the words, "planned, firm, gentle touch."

The thing to grasp is this: touch has to be planned, expected, and not sudden. ADHD sufferers are not fond of unasked-for physical or mental interruptions. They'll need to know they're going to get a massage. Then, your touch should be firm enough not to irritate, and slow enough not to over-stimulate and rush them. Some sufferers like quiet music, but never complex, or too loud; others prefer not to have any other focus: your hands will be more than enough. Aromatherapy might be another really good suggestion to combine with massage, but remember that some ADHD-sufferers' sense of smell is very sensitive too.

It's not all bad to be sensitive. Sensitive people can react really well to stimuli; they can also give a really good massage to you, for the same reason. This is a two-way communication, after all.

More hyperactive people with ADHD need more vigorous, active massage to get them to sit still. They might react better with a firmer touch. However, touch calms them down and they may enjoy gentler treatment once that's achieved. Your partner might have to be a bit more patient than most people to get to a state of calm, but don't be put off, it will happen.

I hope you are inspired to try some free, easy-to-do, simple exercises in giving and receiving physical touch that can help you to enjoy each other's presence.

Stop Being a "Critical Parent":

Do not:

- *Avoid talking about "ADHD" because that's an "un-pleasant" word.* ADHD is part of the truth for your partner and for you as well; he or she isn't a little kiddie who you have to hide things from. It's not being negative to call the problem by its name, when you're communicating with your partner about what you both are going to do about it. But don't ever try to shame your partner for suffering from ADHD.

- *Be a harsh judge and critical of his or her efforts.* Don't be negative if your partner doesn't always meet your agreed targets or outcomes. If life at home is still messy, or things are still forgotten, acknowledge that they are doing their best, even when that might not be your best. Allow them time to get things right.

- *Evaluate your partner like a teacher or trainer.* You aren't there to show him or her all the negatives, to get the fastest results. When you talk together afterwards about how effective plans and activities were, don't sound like a tennis coach saying, "OK, you won the first game, but then you lost the next one because you're just not getting a spin on the ball. You'll always go out if you try that move with a flat whack of the racquet." Think of yourself as the close friend watching the match from the best seat. Encourage, cheer, be excited. Gasp with horror if you must, but only because you want him or her to win. Why not explain this to your partner in these or similar words?

- *Accept excuses with a shrug.* Having ADHD makes many simple jobs hard. However, your encouragement is not the same as accepting it when he or she just gives up. Your partner has to persevere. When you remind him or her not to give up, do it with gentle encouragement, and give praise for what they have achieved so far. Tell your partner you understand that it's difficult.

- *Demand too much of your partner.* You may set goals for him or her, even push them to agree to the goals with you, but the expectations are too high. It is especially important not to put pressure on him or her that could lead to a train of worries and obsessive thoughts. People without ADHD may be unaware of how rapidly their partner can think of possibilities and see problems. It's potentially a great gift (I want you to know that and communicate it to your partner), but to slow them down and get their focus back, say exactly what needs to be done, and put aside other secondary aspects. Accept that the results might not be what you and your partner had hoped for.

- *Lecture him or her.* Try practicing your words if you are going to say something that is a criticism, and see if it can be made to sound loving and not controlling.

- *Try to control your partner.* Controlling people doesn't

work; they resent it. You need to hold yourself back, to motivate your partner instead.

- *Be emotionally forceful.* Trying to be forceful is going to provoke your partner into being emotional in return. Take time out when you feel angry, frustrated or disappointed, and come back when you can talk with less angst and more self-control.

- *Be impulsive yourself.* You know your partner will tend to act impulsively. Are you impulsive yourself? If you are, you need to try to be fair and rational. Just as he or she must learn to use reason to regulate feeling, so must you. You are a partner and friend, not a professor. Teach patience by example, not by saying, "You have to be patient!"

- *Label them.* Labels trap people into behaving in the way they're labelled. Being compassionate means giving your partner the opportunity to grow and change.

- *Use the word, "never", as in, "You never get that right", or, "You've never tried."* This also traps people in hopelessness. It's hostile and usually unfair (Really? Not even once?). Things don't have to remain the same.

- *Use the words, "Just do it..."* What is straightforward for you is just not straightforward for someone with

ADHD. This may be hard for you to understand, but realize that they also don't know why things are difficult, only that they are. Asking them, "But why did you forget it?" will make them want to reply, "If I knew, I wouldn't have forgotten it, would I?"

- *Leave them to finish everything because you "don't want him/her to become too dependent."* It's true that you shouldn't keep taking over, but there is nothing wrong with helping at times. It's what neurotypical people do for each other on many occasions, and they don't usually assume the help shouldn't have been needed.

- *Try to manage all your responsibilities on your own.* Parents shouldn't need outside help, should they? Of course they do! You aren't Superwoman or Superman, and you're not a parent to your partner, in any case. Get help from friends, a therapist, family members. Maybe just someone you can cry in front of! You'll feel better for having got it out.

Don't Forget to Look After Yourself

I said it before: one challenge of trying to look after someone is that you forget to look after yourself. Don't allow yourself to feel guilty when you know you are doing your best. Don't allow other people to do it to you either.

Make time to communicate with sympathetic members of your family, or your partner's. They still need you, and you need them; they can be a great source of help. It goes without saying, however, that you need to look after yourself by keeping quietly away from toxic and selfish family members from either side.

One of the ways you can feel better is to make a mental list. Think of all the things you like and love about your partner. The things that drew you to him or her. Be thankful for those good qualities – and don't forget to tell your partner about them!

PART 4 - WHEN THINGS GET BAD

CHAPTER 9: IDENTIFYING THE SIGNS OF ABUSE

Most of this book has been written to help people who are trying to improve, help, or just save their relationships. However, I need to acknowledge, as will you, that a certain number of partners with ADHD can be abusive, sometimes dangerously so. At the same time, the weaknesses of other partners who suffer from ADHD could leave them vulnerable to your own frustrated or angry behavior. It can be tempting to try to control, manipulate and retaliate against someone who's horribly difficult to live with, especially if their attitude isn't helping.

So you're going to read some advice to help you to recognize if you are, or have been, abused in your relationship. You will also be able to check your own side of the interaction to make sure you haven't been trying to pay back in kind. I will explain how emotional abuse happens, so you can protect yourself, and your children and loved ones where relevant.

When a partner is consistently, gravely and deliberately abusive, then improving, helping, or saving your relationship just isn't going to be possible. In that case, you have the next chapter where I deal with divorcing or separating from someone who has ADHD.

But first, it's time to look at what kinds of abuse may happen, how abusers work, and how to recognize emotional and psychological manipulation in particular.

The most obvious kind of abuse is from lack of emotional control. A significant number of people with ADHD lose their temper seriously and verbally abuse others. Their insults can be very personal, and they find it more difficult, on average, to express anger assertively. That means either they try to silence themselves and keep it in, or they explode. Years of this behavior at regular intervals is exhausting and disheartening for any non-ADHD partner.

It's true that we all have arguments with those we live with and love. However, families become dysfunctional when it's no longer a passing, here-and-there occurrence but a regular, bad habit. Lack of emotional control can cause someone with ADHD to start arguments – and not your average arguments... Shouting or tears can start up without warning, often out of proportion to the apparent crisis. When children are present, the effects of habitual arguing are going to be serious for them if they don't get some kind of protection and guidance.

Physical violence is more common among younger men who have ADHD, and are in a relationship. Though researchers would like more statistics to prove this, counselors and therapists mostly agree. The Pittsburgh ADHD Longitudinal Study compared individuals with ADHD diagnosed in childhood and individuals without. The findings show that those who had ADHD diagnosed were more verbally violent, and more physically violent, than controls (i.e. non-ADHD young men).

If you are treated with violence, you must get help. If physical aggression is repeated, and looks as if it will become a habit, you need to leave for your own safety. While it may be true that a spouse or partner with ADHD doesn't mean to lose control, it's too grave a problem to ignore.

Emotional, psychological manipulation and violence (yes, I call it violence) is more subtle, varied, and complicated. I think it's as bad as physical violence, so later in the chapter I'm going to give it the focus and importance it deserves.

Before that, it is time to stop this train of thought for a moment, and ask yourself if you are being abusive to your partner.

Signs You May Be Abusive to Your Partner

When your partner shouts or cries and screams at you, do you shout, or cry, or scream back? Are your words hostile and insulting? Do you ever say things like, "You're a disgusting slob!", "You're a spoilt little girl who wants others to do everything for her!", or "You arrogant bastard!"? If your partner hears words like that from you on a regular basis then you're abusing him or her. Some sufferers of ADHD are extremely sensitive to rejection, and will feel wounded very easily. Think how much worse this will be when they get verbal attacks and insults.

You have to control your own temper with rational analysis of exactly why you are angry, taking time to go away before speaking, and speaking about problems when you are not feeling heightened emotion. If you can't control yourself as a neurotypical, how is your partner with ADHD supposed to control him- or herself?

You will know if you've hit, thrown things at, punched or otherwise hurt your partner. If you have, you've abused them, period. If you are a woman, and you've done it to a man, I don't think it's an exception. It's not OK.

If you have manipulated or intimidated him or her, this is also abusive. More on this later.

Even if you're being abused by someone else, abusing them in retaliation isn't good, and only invites further retaliation in return. A more passive or introverted character may not retaliate, but will be damaged all the same. I hope and trust that the very fact you ask yourself if you've ever been abusive to your partner is a positive sign that you haven't, or are going to stop it if you have been. I hope this book will help you neither to abuse, nor be abused.

You would also do well to ask whether your spouse or partner is being abused by someone else. If it is happening, it can only influence your relationship.

Why would people with ADHD be likely to suffer abuse from others? It's quite simple, really. We know that:

- people with ADHD have low self-esteem;

- they find it harder to keep friends or stay close to family, so are easier to isolate – which abusers want to do;

- sometimes people with ADHD tend to assume the best in others. At any rate, they often take words at face value and don't realize they've been lied to, or that communication's distorted;

- they are more vulnerable emotionally, prone to flights of temper, of depression. They're more untrusting of their feelings, even when feeling tells them "something's not right here";

- these people lose their jobs often, get paid less on average than neurotypicals, which often makes them financially dependent;

- they often feel guilty: manipulative types use guilt as a lever to get things out of them;

- they need organizers, so abusers can hide the money, the details of organizing etc. from ADHD victims.

I now want to return to the theme of emotional and psychological abuse. Human beings with ADHD problems may find it harder to be abusive than neurotypicals. However, that's not always the case. Remember that they can be intelligent and resourceful. Their rambling minds can be inventive. Don't forget their hyper-focusing tendency: if you are put under that gaze, and you've angered them, disappointed them... They have a habit of idolizing those they fall in love with, then of being deeply disappointed and depressed when the "honeymoon effect" wears off. It may be true that he or she doesn't notice things in conversation or expressed emotion as easily or as quickly as you do. However, with time and experience, your partner will notice nonetheless. He or she may realize with fury, disgust, and disappointment that you've hidden some knowledge or fact from them. It may be really tempting to hide that awareness from you, pretend still not to know, and start taking revenge. People who know humiliation and frustration from experience might know well how humiliation and frustration "work." Partners with ADHD, although maybe a minority, can and do abuse their non-ADHD partners.

Are You Being Abused Mentally by Your Partner With ADHD?

Educating others about psychological abuse involves making you aware of what's called "gaslighting". This term takes its name from the play and well-known 1940s Hollywood adaptation titled *Gas Light*. In this Victorian-era story, Jack and Bella are husband and wife. When Jack goes out in the evening, and Bella is alone, she thinks she hears footsteps in the empty flat above them in their tenement, and the gas-powered lamps in their home start going dim. The flat above was the home of a wealthy woman who died: Is it haunted? When she tells Jack, he tries make his wife think she's imagining the noises, that the gas lights are actually all right, and that she's having delusions. This strategy is successful: Bella becomes confused and her nerves collapse.

The ruse unravels, however, when a policeman visits Bella and tells her that they're investigating the unsolved murder of the old lady who lived above. The motive seems to have been the theft of her valuable jewelry. Soon, Bella realises the truth. Jack gets into the empty flat and walks around, because he's trying to find the hidden jewels. In order to see better, he has the lights there turned on full. Because the gas is shared between the apartments in the building, this makes the pressure drop in Jack and Bella's home, thus making the light grow dimmer. Once she understands, Bella exposes Jack as the murderer, and he's arrested.

Gaslighting is a hidden attempt to make the victim think he or she is forgetful, unable to cope, confused, even mad, or unsuited to take any responsibility. Jack, in this story, makes a careful, psychological effort to control and weaken Bella by denying the truth of her experiences. It can also be a denial of the victim's beliefs about something; the goal is that the victim loses self-confidence and becomes confused. The reason for the abuser to want confusion is because confused, stressed, and unhappy people are easier to manipulate. The "gaslighter" wants to make the victim dependent on him or her, possibly so that the victim does something to the gaslighter's advantage. Jack is desperate to hide a murder, but the motives for gaslighting can be for any self-interest: to take revenge, or to compensate for feelings of inferiority (common to many ADHD sufferers).

Gaslighting can be combined with physical violence and verbal abuse and insult. It doesn't have to be, though, and some of the most dangerous of abusers do it without their victims knowing what's going on, for a long time. It's an attempt to deny your reality, as the victim: to deny the validity of your thoughts and feelings, and your memory. You might be told a lie about some event, so that you try to remember how it was. Because the lie will be repeated (often not exactly in the same form...) you will keep going back to your memory. Subtly, then, you will not be sure if you remembered correctly. You will have all the different versions you heard from your gaslighting abuser memorized as well, and the constant "re-remembering" can lead to confusion.

Other times an abuser challenges and opposes, mocks or reacts with sorrow, when you recall something. Your remembering may be ridiculed, even, or denied with violent anger. In the same way, you will be driven back to examining your own memory, pressured to question it, so that you start to doubt yourself. In the case of someone with ADHD, who probably has a bad short-term memory, you may wonder why they'd try this. I mentioned feelings of inferiority, common to many victims of psychological conditions that affect performance, and these would be a likely cause of resentment.

There are many different kinds of gaslighting, and the degree to which a victim is affected varies. This could depend on your own resistance to mental pressure, or what the abuser wants from you.

One of our natural supports and constant reality checks is our network of friends and family. Other people comment on what we've experienced, or go through it themselves. We ask them for opinions, and they ask us. Manipulative people of all kinds, gaslighters included, seek to isolate their target. When someone's partner angers or alienates their family, causing them to visit less often, causes or worsens conflict between them and their family-members, or does the same to friends, it's done to cut the victim off. Other people might agree with and support the victim, and that would act against the gaslighting. Manipulative people are drawn to lonely, shy and traumatized personalities, precisely because they are easier to use and abuse in their isolation.

What sort of things do gaslighters do and say, exactly? Imagine you said to your spouse, "You said you wanted us to stay in a bed and breakfast because you're uncomfortable staying with my mother." He or she replies, "I never said that!" Those are the infamous words gaslighters often use. You must, they tell you, be thinking of someone else, of some other situation – or maybe you are lying.

Lying is part of all gaslighting, from blatant lies to subtle distortions or hints. You could be asked questions in such a way that it looks as if your abuser doesn't know the answer, when you believe that he or she does. You may be the one who is accused of lying, when you disagree with what they say. A malicious ADHD sufferer might use these tactics to confuse you so much that a shared arrangement fails, making you look equally forgetful and incompetent. Don't forget: people with ADHD might have bad short-term memory, but some of them have very good long-term memory. In any case, if they really want to do something, they can and will put effort into remembering it.

One can identify basic strategies and characteristics of a gaslighter:

- The degree of manipulation could be so severe as to try to destroy you, e.g. drive you to commit suicide. Alternatively, it could be just a slight twist to keep you under more control, or a long-term use of you to provide money, attention, love, fame, household help, or anything at all;

- The manipulation could be open, even public, combined with verbal and/or, physical violence. Or it could be a sort of severe criticism in private when you're alone together, while he or she is always polite to you when there are other people around. On the other side of the scale, it may be totally hidden. The abuser may put great effort into looking, to you, like a lover and helper, while he or she breaks down your self-confidence and your ability to handle stress.

- Lying is always a part of the strategy. It varies from open and arrogant untruths through to twisted facts, all the way to subtle suggestions and questions that are not framed as statements. This last version is called "innuendo."

- Denial is also an essential part of the strategy; anything from rages and rants to half-yawned "no"s with a shake of the head. If you were to accuse your partner of having an affair, he might scream at you, shouting, "How dare you accuse me of having an affair! Are you trying to destroy my good standing with my family?" Or else, he might roll his eyes and say, "Oh, really; that's absolutely ridiculous."

- Gaslighters use a lot of counter-accusation. So, in the case of marital infidelity again, a man might confront his wife with the accusation that she's been seen eating out with a work colleague at an expensive restaurant. Then she shouts back, "You're just saying that because you're the one who's having an affair! I know you are! I've seen her phone number in your phone, on your call logs. She's one of your customers!"

- Being two-faced, is another tactic. This could involve, for example, angry, critical behavior in the morning. Then, in the afternoon, the abuser might come back and greet the victim brightly, and start chatting pleasantly. It's as if the other type of behavior never happened. The victim will often neglect to follow up on an incident, perhaps to keep the peace. The abuser just gets away with it. If the victim does remind him or her, the abuser can just use one of the other aforementioned tactics.

Do you recognize your partner in any of this? It may be hard to spot at first, and rather unsettling for you to admit. However, if you are being gaslighted, it's something you need to know. You may not be crazy, after all...

If you really are being systematically confused, there may be a clear reason, such as your partner having an affair, or hiding expenses from you, or a drug habit. If you give him or her an opportunity to explain what is wrong, and you don't get a good reason, or just denial, and gaslighting continues, then you will have to take stock.

You need to protect yourself if you've been gaslighted by your partner – or anyone, for that matter. There are many good guides to dealing with the effects of gaslighting, and to help victims recognize what's been happening to them. Quite clearly, someone who systematically gaslights you, isolates you from other people, or uses them to attack you (that's another tactic of gaslighters), doesn't love you. Could I put it more clearly than that?

The kind of person who gaslights others, uses them, and lies, is narcissistic or sociopathic. Such people don't do this just because they've had a bad day. The evidence points to manipulative, narcissistic people becoming so in their childhood or teenage years. Early adulthood, at the latest. They react to some suffering or disappointment by deciding that the world and everyone in it is junk, and that they are going to live for themselves alone, using people for what they can get out of them. These are mostly not people with ADHD; but since people with ADHD are just human beings with ADHD, they can be among them.

You have to get out of such a relationship. If you are in a manipulative relationship like this, it's almost 100-percent certain that your partner was toxic from the beginning. Manipulative liars don't tell you on your third date, or just before you make love the first time, "Oh, by the way, I'm a manipulative little gold digger who's going to use you for all I can get out of you, and then I'll abuse you and maybe throw you away." No, they hide their attitudes, their previous relationships, and any incriminating evidence, and try to stay on their best behavior. So don't feel guilty for falling for their tricks – just plan to get out.

Is there any point telling your partner that you know they gaslight you? I don't believe so – what's the point? Given their habit of counter-accusation, don't bother. Such gaslighting types are likely to turn around and accuse you of gaslighting!

Your defense is, first of all, not to attack. Don't abuse in turn. Narcissistic people, gaslighters, are by nature very given to revenge. You have to react with outward calm, no matter how angry or disappointed you feel. For example, if you are told that you didn't pay the electricity bill, when you know you did, because your partner never used to; don't react with shock or visible sadness. Just say something like, "Yes, I'm sure I did. I remember doing it on Wednesday." When your abusive partner says, "No, you didn't go out on Wednesday; you went out on Thursday, and you didn't go to the town center," don't bother to challenge it vigorously. Perhaps you can say, as you walk away, "I'm sure I did go out on Wednesday."

Being visibly upset, shouting, or loudly declaring that someone is not telling the truth – even though they are lying – only gives an abuser what psychologists call "narcissistic supply." It's proof that they are bothering you – and bothering you is one of their goals, because it's a tool to confuse you and make you passive. It can be useful to calmly use the words, "At least you know we've spoken about this."

In the meantime, find some sympathetic people to listen to you. Keep notes about important facts – as you've tried to get your partner to do. Get all the advice online you can.

Some people with ADHD aren't so toxic, but they still try to manipulate and make unacceptable excuses. Think of some- one who cheats on you, has an affair, takes banned drugs, and so on, and says to your face, "But I didn't mean it. I did it because I have ADHD." I have mentioned that such actions that endanger your relationship, or their life, or are a serious problem, and can't be brushed aside with a flippant excuse. Such excuses sound as if your partner has no will to change, or be responsible. Responsibility is needed to grow personally and to manage ADHD, from their side as much as from yours.

CHAPTER 10: ENDING A RELATIONSHIP WITH A PARTNER WHO HAS ADHD

There are times when a relationship breaks down completely – or was never healthy to begin with. If this describes your situation, I acknowledge the difficulty and pain that you must be in, and offer you guidance on how to divorce, or separate from, someone who has ADHD. If it's the case that your partner is the one who wants to leave you, most of the strategies are very similar.

Three "Marriage- and Relationship-Killing" Scenarios

I can think of three deep and important reasons why you might have to divorce your partner or separate legally. First of all, you might have started the relationship without really knowing what your partner was like, or without your partner really knowing you. You might have decided to share your life and most intimate concerns too soon; you might have married without really knowing who your spouse was; you might have started living together and only then got to know quite what you'd let yourself in for.

This isn't an accusation. People can and do make mistakes, and make promises of commitment too soon, without knowing what they're committing themselves to. I can understand absolutely that somebody with ADHD is, by virtue (or is it vice?) of being impulsive and prone to hyper-focus, likely to rush into marriage, or engagement, or to moving in, and hoping all will be well. I have stated clearly that for reasons beyond their awareness and control, some sufferers of ADHD are very deceptive when they are falling in love and experiencing the newness and excitement... of you. You won't see problems such as their exhaustion, forgetfulness, hyper-sensitivity, boredom, distraction, impulsivity and moodiness, violent or dangerous behavior, substance abuse, or their disorganization and craving for excitement, until later.

Yes: not marrying, not getting engaged, not moving in too soon, is good advice. But what if you've already done it? We can't re-write the past, and I don't condemn you if you acted too quickly. Instead, I'd like you to accept that when you don't know some really, deeply significant fact – such as suffering from ADHD – regarding someone you marry or otherwise commit yourself to, through no fault of yours, that promise is not really as binding as it would have been if you had known or understood it. Sometimes you read advice that says, "Pack your bags and move on." It's never that simple. However, don't feel that you're doing something totally wicked and irresponsible, if this is the reality of your situation. You may need to do it, and in any case, you'll need to get over your traumatic experiences.

The second reason why you'd be right to consider divorce would be if your partner's in denial of his or her condition. Did your partner, at the beginning, deliberately hide this extremely important fact about himself or herself, having been told about their ADHD, knowing all too well about its effects on his or her life? Did the symptoms come out undeniably, and you've talked about it with him or her, but they refuse to consider therapy or any kind of medication, or help?

The third reason is the most tragic for you. In this case, he or she never really meant to make a serious commitment to you, to love you and cherish you. That may be especially true if he or she is narcissistic and manipulating. Usually, such personalities make a promise to you and undertake a responsibility for you, and pledge faithfulness to you, that they have no intention of keeping.

These considerations hold true for any relationship that fails totally and needs to be broken off. You see, it comes back to the fact that a person who has ADHD is a human being... who happens to have ADHD.

People living with ADHD are not automatically exempt from responsibility. Sometimes, and in some ways, ADHD does make responsibility hard to bear, or in moments even impossible. Yet they aren't all innocent victims by definition, since there are things they can and should do once they have awareness of their condition. Most people with ADHD are not liars and villains who use their symptoms as a cover to manipulate, but some are.

From that, it follows that some of them have a serious problem that is no fault of their own, and which they may be somewhat willing to challenge and adapt to. A problem you didn't see at the beginning of the relationship. So you try to help them because you love them, and still after years, even, it may be utterly exhausting and stressful, perhaps a financial and parenting disaster. This struggle may last for life.

Yet there are also those who give up, live in denial, and don't want to try to change or learn. They may try to play the child with you, plead with you, put you and themselves in danger, or expect you to tolerate behavior that could include having an affair. They may say they'll commit suicide if you leave, but when you stay, they use you again and don't try to get help. This, and other aspects of their emotional instability is actually gaslighting, although I prefer to call it emotional sabotage.

Others decide that not only are they not interested in changing, but that the way forward is to get back at the people, and the world, that dealt them a bad hand, so to say. They decide to use others for their benefit; if they acknowledge they have ADHD in any way, then you are just there to help them with it until such time as an impulse that's too good to miss comes along. When you r partner is someone like this latter type, your relationship is doomed. This follows from what I said about gaslighting and psychological abuse. Such an attitude manifests itself with time, and results in lies, malicious manipulation, hostile behavior, and cold-blooded selfishness. Such a narcissistic or sociopathic attitude does exist in some people with ADHD, and to be totally fair, a greater number who don't have ADHD at all. I don't believe that somebody like this can make a valid or binding promise: they just want something out of you or others. This is a toxic relationship that you would be advised to distance yourself from.

Considerations With Divorce or Legal Separation

As with any other solution to personal challenges and problems, leaving a bad relationship in the best way will hurt, but it heals. Or rather, it will heal, but it's going to hurt.

The most frequent reasons for wanting a divorce from someone with ADHD are precisely their emotional lack of control, and fighting with you. For most sufferers, that is exactly what will manifest if you initiate the proceedings, and in the negotiations, anyway, if they do. People with ADHD are variable, but high-conflict individuals are understandably more likely to be those involved in a divorce or legal proceedings. People with gaslighting personalities, or who at least use some of these tactics, are also prone to retaliation and revenge. Their unpleasant side is sure to be triggered if you must oppose them on some matter, or simply are leaving them. I hope you see from the previous sections that if you stay, you're going to be traumatized in any case, so don't give up.

It's important to be prepared. You need to protect yourself by distancing, so you can begin to recover and handle the situation better. To be kind to your ex-partner, I admit he or she will need some kind of help in the organizing of what is a practical and legal challenge. That person may continue to be you with the help of a lawyer and a counselor, unless your ex-partner is so toxic that the lawyer will have to be the go-between.

You have to be clear to yourself, first. You must realize that you can't change your partner, only manage them better. Don't take the blame, or allow yourself to feel responsible for everything that's gone wrong. Neither should you try to be the logical, problem-solving "Parent," bristling with bright ideas that they must follow.

Your choice of lawyer, and of any counseling or psychological help, is very important for getting a better and more peaceable outcome. If you can find a lawyer experienced in working with people who have ADHD, so much the better. It is vital that he or she understands your crisis, and that he or she should understand your partner. You also need a therapist or counselor: your therapist's advice and support will help to keep you focused, remain strong, and react logically and fairly, despite temptation to let your emotions rule.

If your partner is in denial, this is the first hurdle. Has he or she had any kind of evaluation, and if so, any treatment, either medical or psychological? A lawyer can help you motivate your partner to do this. Point out calmly that the courts want to see evidence of something serious being done about an alleged problem. It works against someone with the symptoms of ADHD, if they refuse to seek help. They may have restricted custody of children, or other conditions imposed on them, but don't phrase it like that yourself. Say briefly that you are told it will be in his or her best interests to do what is advised, just as it is for you to have a licensed therapist who can evaluate you.

Specific ADHD-Related Problems Your Partner May Have During and After Divorce

Some of these will be the same, familiar ones you had during your relationship, but there will likely be some new additions:

- Furious outbursts and maybe floods of tears and hysterics

- Promises made to control these emotional states, but which the extra stress breaks

- Making agreements and not abiding by them, sometimes just out of confusion or forgetfulness

- The familiar disorganization: so he or she misses appointments, loses forms and doesn't submit paperwork, doesn't complete said paperwork correctly, is late because of procrastination and so on

- Losing control of his or her personal life, becoming paralyzed and inactive, or falling prey to dangerous or thrill-seeking escapism;

- Lying about details, to cover his or her disorganization;

- Not looking after your children, if you have them, nor paying for them, or forgetting to collect them when custody is shared.

The Right Attitude to Maintain Through the "Storm"

Quite a lot of the techniques I mentioned for living with and helping someone who has ADHD are actually also relevant when distancing yourself from them. This is because they're managing strategies.

- Don't respond to emotional outbursts and personal, verbal attacks with hostility or too much emotion. Without sounding cold or unfriendly, just be very firm and keep your words to a minimum.

- Use what conflict-management experts call "E.A.R ." communications. That stands for communicating with Empathy, Attention and Respect. If he or she was sick, for example, then say that you're sorry to hear that, and hope that he or she gets better. Talk to your partner as someone who matters. You may even give praise for an achievement, such as, "Congratulations for winning that singing contest."

You might get it thrown in your face, e.g. "Why are you so interested in the contest? You're supposed to be divorcing me." Don't react to that in kind. Perhaps you can say, "I'm still happy for you. We just need to sort out some arrangements." On the other hand, you might have the "game" played on you, of "I'm so nice and sympathetic; look how kind I'm being to him/her." If you get that, just be polite in return, but don't be drawn into a discussion.

- Draw boundaries and set consequences, with your legal help. It mustn't sound like a retaliation. Just say that, for example, "We arranged that if you do x, I will do y." "You needed to do x by such a date, but you haven't, so I must do y." Don't try to motivate your ex-partner with words such as, "You really should do that, it's much better than..." and don't argue or explain. Always keep your promises and do your duties.

- A lot of modern communication takes place electronically. Never mind a steering wheel – some people go totally extreme and obsessive when they're behind the screen of a computer. The insults one reads on the internet today are saddening in their intensity and sheer volume. So if you or your lawyer gets streams of insulting communication, and yet you must read it and reply, do it in a brief and controlled way. Give only the needed information, be friendly without sounding false, and be very clear and unbending about what's been promised and arranged. Don't lecture or sound critical.

- Where a relationship is not so bad that communication is still possible, you can continue to talk to your ex-partner, by phone or maybe in person, to do the planning together that you used to do, if you achieved that. In the case of custody of children, this is particularly important. In the situation of breakup, you do need to step back a bit, but you can make occasional reminders, or ask for an honest opinion of how he or she feels about the daily organizing of some very specific points.

- On the other hand, where you've been physically abused or seriously psychologically affected, then contact must be solely through a lawyer, family therapist or specialized social or legal worker. You may need to change phone numbers, block your ex-partner from conversations, or leave groups you were in together. Again, a good legal adviser and a counselor can show how to do this, or to handle the strictly necessary contacts, if any.

Strategies That Manipulative or Hysterical People Use, and How to Respond

There are many of them, but I highlight these ones, with some suggestions. Your case may vary, but there should be some help here.

"If I go for therapy, will you take me back?" This sounds reasonable, but it's actually emotional bargaining. Assuming that your spouse has been in denial, or stopped medication, or failed to take any other action they needed to do for their own benefit

as well as yours, they do indeed need therapy. However, you can't make it a condition. People go to therapy or doctors for their own needs, not to earn some kind of "brownie points." In this case, I would reply that, "You need to go for therapy, that's certain. Anyone with ADHD needs help. We will only know afterwards if it's right for us to get back together. I can't make a promise about what I don't know, and you don't either." Be firm, but kind.

"I'll kill myself if you leave." This is similar but it's worse. It's emotional blackmail. You still need to be very firm, as you are kind. Perhaps you say, "I know you feel that you want to die, because you can't organize your life and it seems too much. I was helping you, and I will carry on helping you, even if it's best for us that I don't stay with you. You need professional help, and I'm not a professional. Of course I don't want you to die; but it won't get better until you get counseling and try medication/unless you carry on with counseling and medication. Think of our struggles and arguments: I couldn't solve the problems for you. You have to work with them. The reason I'm saying this is because I care about you, not because I don't." There is a risk of ADHD sufferers committing suicide, so don't rubbish it. However, they're trying to make you feel bad, and that's no good for anybody. Not you, and not him or her.

"I'll turn the children against you." This is emotional terrorism. Without losing your temper, you have to be absolutely firm

here. If something like this is said over the phone, it may help to record it. You have to be clear that your problems are your problems, and your partner's are theirs – not the children's. The children need love, and not to learn how to hate. Say, "I understand that you may be upset with me, and I with you, but you can't use children to try to get back at me. I don't want to hurt you, and I don't want the kids to get hurt either. You need to get help if you feel this way. I need help to make sure that I treat the kids the way I should." Such words certainly indicate a serious problem, and you need to talk to a therapist about them, and inform your lawyer. Treating children as weapons is not psychologically stable, and could and should affect custody. However, don't threaten your spouse – it's just an incentive for them to threaten you even more.

There are many more less pathological but infuriating tactics that overemotional ADHD sufferers sometimes use. Your approach needs to be logical, quiet and confident, and yet kind. But firm! What you are doing is steering a middle course between the rocks of your partner's denial or hostility on one hand, and their overemotional response to protect what they see as a threat to their existence, on the other.

With time, managing your ex-spouse or partner will grow easier. You will have learnt these strategies by heart, and you need to be realistic that it's unlikely that you can stop them any time soon. Accept the battle, but allow yourself to put more focus on the often-neglected side of ADHD in relationships: the non-ADHD partner's experiences and needs. You need to live your own life better and recover emotionally, even physically, from the strain. That recovery is the topic of the next chapter.

CHAPTER 11: WHAT SHOULD YOU DO AFTER ENDING A RELATIONSHIP WITH A PARTNER WHO HAS ADHD?

If you've had to go through a separation because you had a partner with ADHD who you couldn't stay with despite your best efforts, or if you've had a partner who suffers from ADHD who decided to separate from you, you need to "debrief." Relationship breakdown is a traumatic experience. Like veterans from a war, some kind of sorting it out, coming to terms with it, and getting over feelings of fear, anger and helplessness is called for.

First of all, ask yourself if there is anything about your ex-partner, or about your experience, that you are in denial about.

Whatever the feelings were, whatever you did or didn't do, whatever he or she did or didn't do, accept it as a fact. If your partner had more of a problem than you cared to admit for some years, accept this. Come to terms with it to feel peace of mind. Was your partner, is he or she still, in denial of ADHD? If that is the case, and if you and others have tried to show your partner that this is their problem, to no avail, accept that you can't control them. Accept that you will manage any remaining arrangements (child support, settlements, alimony, visiting time, etc.) and let that be enough.

Secondly, you need to forgive yourself, and also your partner. This word, "forgive", can sound so glib and complacent. What I mean is not a feeling, but a decision to let go of what you can't change, and to persevere with what you can.

Forgive yourself too: there are many feelings that may arise in your situation, all impacted by who you are, what kind of a person your ex is, the length of your relationship, whether any children are involved, and so forth. You may feel relief, and yet feel guilty at the same time. You may feel bitter and angry that effort, life, and love was wasted, yet still be able to feel some love for your ex-partner. You may be able to think of activities you want to focus on now, but sometimes find yourself running out of energy. Why do you feel such contrary emotions and desires, you might ask? It's a response to a trauma, something rather like the fluctuating, extreme emotions ADHD causes your partner to have.

However, even when you did the wrong things, playing the "Parent," shouting back, "dumping" things to be remembered on him or her when you reminded them – forgive yourself. If your partner's ADHD was undiagnosed, you didn't know better either. If you did know, and just got so irritated and baited that you were the one to explode verbally – it's in the past now. Choose to learn from your experiences; and realize that feeling shame about your side of the breakdown isn't going to motivate you to start being more assertive and positive.

Knowing the reason your ex struggled or caved in to temptation can help you to feel less bitter. Knowing about and understanding their past treatment by others, and their feelings of frustrated, helpless pain; knowing that they sensed something was wrong with them, but not knowing what, shows you why they feel so angry and disappointed sometimes. Even if you were so unfortunate to have married a narcissistic person, with vindictive and hate-filled attitudes... forgive them.

Forgive, because you need to let go. Your bitterness will hurt you more than them. Forgiveness is not trying to say that someone didn't do you wrong; many victims of ADHD use personal, inflammatory, even gaslighting language when they are out of emotional control. These aren't necessarily the anti-social or narcissistic ones, but the damage they inflict is still significant. However, what's done is done. If it wasn't meant, forgive it. If it was, forgive it. You have every right to protect yourself from some people, your children more again. However, putting insults and dangerous behavior, violence and debt, behind you, is part of forgiving. Forgiving isn't excusing.

If all your financial problems were over, if settlements, agreements, and child custody issues were solved, you would still feel anger and bitterness if you didn't let go and forgive your ex-partner. So I urge you to do it, to say the words, "I forgive you" to them in your mind. You could even say it in person, though in the case of a manipulating, dangerous type you need to distance yourself from, I would make an exception. Even in that case, I'd ask you to carry on saying those words to yourself.

Guilt is a common problem for non-ADHD spouses after a marriage breaks up: any relationship with a sufferer of this condition, that fails, may provoke intense feelings of shame. You realize that you had someone with a severe and lifelong challenge that they never asked for, who needs help – and you've left them. Or, they've left you: either way you feel as if you've deserted a victim.

If you feel this way, remind yourself of what steps you took to understand your partner, to see the world as he or she sees it, and to be compassionate. If you didn't know about the diagnosis of ADHD until now when it's over, then you can't be held accountable for what you didn't know. If you did know, and you tried to help and encourage, tried to make sure that the two of you had professional diagnoses and advice, and your partner still didn't want to change, or admit his or her great need, then you can still refuse to accept guilty feelings. However disappointed you might be, you can rest in the fact that you tried.

It's a sore point: sometimes you need to forgive yourself for having had children with someone. Often the sheer joy of having someone to love and nurture stops this feeling; but some people, some mothers especially, feel such pain and sense of waste at a ruined marriage or similar relationship, and see such a disaster for the children born into it, that they feel guilty for having brought them into the world. Be calm and logical if you feel like this. Don't think of the past and present suffering your children endured, and may do while parents argue and separate. Think of their future... and renew your commitment to giving them unconditional love. There's hope for them, because there's life.

Once they are no longer together with a spouse or partner with ADHD, many people feel intense relief. It may dawn on them just how much energy their ex-partner was consuming out of their common life. If you tried to heal the communication and behavior issues with your partner, but it didn't succeed, you might still be glad that you tried. In that case, there is no need for shame. If your ex-partner lived, or lives, in denial of his or her condition, we know that untreated, unguided ADHD makes life hell for those who suffer it and those who live with them. One can't help but feel relief when you've put some distance between you and their infamous disorganization and stress.

In most cases of divorce, there will be some connection or communication afterwards, especially if you have children together. The words, "put some distance between" are an important way to understand how your life will be from now on. You need space to heal and grow, to move on with your life. However, you can still love your ex-husband or wife, or partner, even when you're not together any more. You can still do some – only some – planning and reviewing of arrangements with them. Don't let yourself be dragged down by the weight of your ex-partner's responsibilities, though. You had to separate to be able to manage your own life, to give your children some peace. Speak and write kindly and firmly, when you come to that.

Regarding children: never let yourself speak badly of your partner in front of them. You may need to say that their mom or dad has problems, and that "we had to move away because that was the only way I could protect you and heal myself." Whatever you say, if you demonstrate kindness, peacemaking efforts, and calm, you will be teaching them how to be loving, instead of showing them that bitterness and judgementalism are acceptable.

Sometimes, after an unpleasant experience that traps you unwillingly, you feel depression and anxiety instead of relief. Kidnap victims and ex-prisoners sometimes report this. Why does that happen? I believe it's because of a defense-mechanism in our psyche. While you are enduring, for example, arguments, debts, forgotten arrangements, dangerous behavior, affairs, or total withdrawal from your ADHD partner, the human mind seems to push away a lot of the trauma and feelings of anger and helplessness. Then, once you, the victim, are able to take some control of the circumstances, especially when that involves leaving them altogether, you feel it all coming up to the surface. Remind yourself that it's just the backlog of emotions that you didn't have the space or time to feel before, and take advantage of the situation to look at them logically. What exactly do you feel? Is it anger, or hopelessness? Is it fear mixed with frustration? What are you afraid of? What did your partner do that still hurts? Then try to look at these issues with the hope that you can deal better with trauma and see more clearly, now that you've left the toxic situation.

Make sure that you continue to get some counseling. You may continue to see the counselor you used to see with your ex-partner, as they know what situation you've come out of. Other people might do well to find a new therapist or lifestyle coach. At any rate, you will benefit greatly from a professional who can help you to see what your confused emotions and thoughts mean, and how to guide them for inner peace. Your lawyer may still be necessary at times, if your partner can't keep to arrangements and agreements, or refuses to.

Every experience, especially bad ones, is an opportunity to learn. You can take away many valuable lessons about life after a failed relationship. They may be of great help if you look for and maybe find someone else to love. However, they will also help you learn about yourself generally. Knowing your weaknesses and strengths is a blessing for you, and anyone who knows you.

To take your mind off any residual negativity, why not take up some new hobby, follow a new interest, or sport? If you were isolated by gaslighting tactics or just by the attention that was demanded of you before, try to connect, or re-connect, with other people. A non-ADHD partners' group is not something you have to leave if your partner leaves you, or you divorce them. Keep in contact with like-minded individuals.

CONCLUSION

I hope you've tried everything you can to make your relationship work. If you're dealing with a new awareness of ADHD in your spouse or partner's life, I hope this book inspires you to understand him or her, and that the two of you can work together to manage the condition. Change and adaptation are possible – in any challenge – when two people admit there is a problem and decide to work at solving it together. Couples where one, or even both, have ADHD can be happy and can thrive. No-one is without their problems, and ADHD is just one of many of life's challenges. It's not a death sentence. If you love someone, you will want to do the best you can, together with them, not just for them.

Being realistic, I have shown you that some couples have a huge challenge. Also, that some victims don't want to confront their painful trial, and end up suffering more pain because of their denial. So do those who love them. Sometimes it's the non-ADHD partner who doesn't want to face facts.

If you've read this book, you are doing something positive to see the truth, so I hope that won't be the case for you. Lastly, as in any human situation, there are some people who don't want anything for anyone except themselves. Some stay stuck in childish selfishness, others will use their adult knowledge and intelligence to carve out an advantage for themselves that manipulates, crushes, uses and destroys other people. In this kind of case you need to separate yourself from the relationship so as to protect yourself and avoid further abuse.

Don't be afraid to ask for advice and get help. I hope you will find people both in person and online who understand that ADHD is not only about little, hyperactive boys who will supposedly "grow out of it." My desire is that you will be able to celebrate the talents and achievements of your partner with ADHD, encouraging and nurturing his or her personal growth, and every brave effort to overcome negativity, and that you will help the one you love to become the person he or she was meant to be.